The True Christian's Love
to the Unseen Christ

by Thomas Vincent
(1634—1678)

Part 1

"If anyone does not love the Lord, that person is cursed!" 1 Corinthians 16:22

To The Reader:

Our Savior sent an epistle from heaven to the church of Ephesus, wherein He reproved her because she had left her first love, and threatened the removal of her candlestick. He would take away her light—if she did not recover her love. By the same hand, at the same time, He sent another epistle to the church of Laodicea, wherein He reproved her lukewarmness, and threatened, because she was neither hot nor cold—that He would spew her out of His mouth, Revelation 2:45 and 3:15-16. And are professors in Britain under no such sin, in no such danger—when some scoff at the flames of love to Christ, like dogs that bark at the moon so far above them; when the most nominal professors are wholly strangers to this love?

The former looking upon it as but a fancy, the latter having it only in the theory and when, among those Christians who love Christ in sincerity, there are so few that know what it is to love Christ with fervor and ardency, when there is so general a decay of love to Christ in the land, Lord, what is likely to become of Britain! Have we not provoked the Lord to take away our candlestick? Have we not provoked the Lord to suffer worse than Egyptian darkness to overspread us again, and cover our light because it shines with such cold beams, because the light of knowledge in the head, is accompanied with so little warmth of love to Christ in the hearts of most Christians? Everyone will fetch water to quench fire in a general conflagration, and surely there is need in a day of such general decay of love to Christ, that some such fetch fire from heaven, and use bellows too; arguments, I mean, to enkindle and blow up the spark of love to Christ which seems so ready to expire.

Reader, the following discourse of the true Christian's love to the unseen Christ, is not finely spun and woven with neatness of wit and language. It is not flourished and set off with a variety of metaphors, hyperboles, rhetorical elegancies, or poetical fancies and fragments. It is not adorned and fringed with the specious show of many marginal quotations, excerpted out of divers authors. The discourse is plain—but the author has endeavored that it might be warm; his design being more to advance his Master, than himself, in your esteem; and if he has less of your praise, so that his Lord may have more of your love— his great end is attained.

The chief part of this discourse concerning the love of Christ is application, and about two thirds of it is exhortation (there being generally in this knowing age more need of excitation than information), where you have a variety of arguments and motives to stir up and provoke us to the love of Christ, together with several directions how to attain this love in the truth and strength of it, and wherein the strength of love to Christ should evidence itself. There is also an appendix added, for further encouragement unto the love of Christ, concerning Christ's manifestation of Himself unto such as love Him. The whole discourse is practical, nothing in it is controversial. All will acknowledge the obligation which Christians have to love Christ; and none will oppose this who are true Christians; none but Turks, Infidels, and Devils, are professedly against it.

That this little book may be blessed by the Lord to be a means to warm and inflame your heart with love to the unseen Christ—is the earnest prayer of,

A hearty well-wisher to your soul,
Thomas Vincent

"You love Him, though you have not seen Him." 1 Peter 1:8

The life of Christianity consists very much in our love to Christ. Without love to Christ, we are as much without spiritual life—as a carcass when the soul is fled from it is without natural life. Faith without love to Christ is a dead faith, and a professor without love to Christ is a dead professor, dead in sins and trespasses. Without love to Christ we may have the name of Christians—but we are wholly without the nature of Christians. We may have the form of godliness—but are wholly without the power of godliness. "Give me your heart!" is the language of God to all people, Proverbs 23:26; and "Give me your love!" is the language of Christ to all His disciples.

Christ knows the command and influence which love to Him, in the truth and strength of it, has; how it will engage all the other affections of His disciples for Him; that if He has their love, their desires will be chiefly after Him. Their delights will be chiefly in Him; their hopes and expectations will be chiefly from Him; their hatred, fear, grief, anger, will be carried forth chiefly unto sin—as it is offensive unto Him. He knows that love will engage and employ for Him, all the powers and faculties of their souls; their thoughts will be brought into captivity and obedience unto Him; their understandings will be employed in seeking and finding out His truths; their memories will be receptacles to retain them; their consciences will be ready to accuse and excuse as His faithful deputies; their wills will choose and refuse, according to His direction and revealed pleasure.

All their senses and the members of their bodies will be His servants. Their eyes will see for Him, their ears will hear for Him, their tongues will speak for Him, their hands will work for Him, their feet will walk for Him. All their gifts and talents will be at His devotion and service. If He has their love—they will be ready to do for Him what He requires. They will suffer for Him whatever He calls them to. If they have much love to Him, they will not think much of denying themselves, taking up His cross, and following Him wherever He leads them. Love to Christ, then, being so essential unto true Christianity, so earnestly looked for by our Lord and Master, so powerfully commanding in the soul and over the whole man, so greatly influential on duty—I have made choice to treat this subject of love to Christ, and my chief endeavor herein shall be to excite and provoke Christians unto the lively and vigorous exercise of this grace of love unto the Lord Jesus Christ, of which incentive there is great and universal need.

The epistle wherein my text lies was written by Peter, the Apostle to the Jews, and is directed "To God's elect, strangers in the world, scattered throughout Pontus, Galatia, Cappadocia, Asia and Bithynia," as in verse one of this chapter. By these strangers we are to understand the scattered Jews who were strangers in these several countries which they inhabited. We read in chapter two of the Acts, that many of these Jews came from these and other countries, unto Jerusalem to worship; and in the Temple, hearing the Apostle speak with several languages, which were of use in the divers places where they lived, and that without instruction from man—but as the Spirit gave them utterance, they were amazed and confounded. Afterward, hearing Peter preach through the wonderful power of the Spirit, three thousand of them were converted by one sermon unto the Christian faith, and were added to the Christian church. When the feast of Pentecost being over, these converted Jews returned into the countries where their several dwellings, families, and callings were; which countries, being heathenish and idolatrous, no doubt but there they met with opposition and suffering upon the account of the Christian religion, which they became zealous professors of, besides what they endured from their own countrymen, or unconverted Jews, who hated Christianity more than the heathens did.

The Apostle seems to have a respect unto these in this epistle wherein he encourages them, under their sufferings for the sake of Christ, by many consolatory arguments. In verse 2, he wished that grace and peace might be multiplied in them and towards them; and then, though their sufferings abounded, their consolation would abound much more. In verses 3, 4, and 5, he blesses God for His abundant mercy towards them in begetting them into a living hope of the glorious and never-fading heavenly inheritance, which was reserved for them through God's infinite grace, and unto which they were reserved and kept through faith by God's infinite power. In the 6th and 7th verses he tells them that, however they were in heaviness through manifold afflictions, which are the world's left-hand temptations— yet he gives them to understand that these afflictions were but for a season. Weeping may endure for a night—but joy comes in the morning. They were needful to humble them, to purify them, to crucify them to the world, to make them conformable to their head, the Lord Jesus Christ; and that they were for the trial of their faith, that the truth of it might appear both to themselves and others, and that the worth of it might appear more precious than gold when it is tried in the fire, which, carrying them through their sufferings, might be found both to their own praise and their Master's honor at the appearing of Jesus Christ.

And then the Apostle takes occasion in the text to speak of their love, which they bore to this Jesus Christ, and of that unspeakable and glorious joy which results from believing in Him although they had no sight of Him, which no trouble or affliction could overwhelm or hinder; "Though you have not seen him, you love him; and even though you do not see him now, you believe in him and are filled with an inexpressible and glorious joy, for you are receiving the goal of your faith, the salvation of your souls." Hence observe:

Doctrine 1. That it is the property and duty of true Christians to love Jesus Christ, whom they have never seen; "Though you have not seen him, you love him."

Doctrine 2. That true Christians believe in an unseen Christ; "even though you do not see him now, you believe in him."

Doctrine 3. That true Christians do, or may, rejoice in believing with unspeakable and glorious joy. "you believe in him and are filled with an inexpressible and glorious joy, for you are receiving the goal of your faith, the salvation of your souls."

Here are three great points:

(1) concerning the love of Christians unto Christ;

(2) concerning the faith of Christians in Christ;

(3) concerning the joy of Christians in believing.

For the present, I shall speak only of the love of Christians unto Christ.

Doctrine: It is the property and duty of true Christians—to love the Lord Jesus Christ, whom they have never seen.

In handling this point, I shall speak—

(1) concerning true Christians who love Jesus Christ;

(2) concerning Jesus Christ whom they have never seen, the object of their love;

(3) concerning the love which they bear unto this unseen Christ;

(4) show that it is the property of true Christians to love Jesus Christ whom they have never seen;

(5) that it is their duty to love Him;

(6) how they ought to love Him;

(7) why they love Him; where I shall give the reasons of the point;

(8) make some use and application.

1. Concerning true Christians whose property it is to love Jesus Christ, whom they have never seen. "Though

you have not seen him, you love him." that is, you are true Christians who are so in reality as well as profession; and of these true Christians who love Christ, the Apostle gives a description in verse 2 where he calls them, "Elect according to the foreknowledge of God the Father, through the sanctifying work of the Spirit, for obedience to Jesus Christ and sprinkling by his blood."

True Christians are elect according to the foreknowledge of God the Father; they are such whom God, according to the counsel of His own will, according to His own purpose and grace, chose from all eternity—to be a holy and peculiar people to Himself, to glorify Him here on earth that they might be glorified by Him hereafter in heaven. And this election evidences itself in the sanctification of the Spirit.

True Christians are sanctified, being separated and set apart from the rest of the world for God's use and service. God has sealed them for Himself, and hereby distinguished them from all others; the motto of this seal is this, "Holiness unto the Lord." See a description of them in this respect, 2 Timothy 2:21, "If a man cleanses himself from the latter, he will be an instrument for noble purposes, made holy, useful to the Master and prepared to do any good work." They are cleansed from the defilement of sin which pollutes and dishonors them: they are vessels unto honor, like those of silver and gold in a great house which are adorned with pearls and precious stones. They are adorned with all sanctifying graces, which are of more worth than the richest jewels, and, hereby they are both beautiful in God's eye, and they are made fit for God's use, being hereby prepared and enabled unto every good work.

This the Apostle prays for on behalf of believers, 1 Thessalonians 5:23, "And the very God of peace sanctify you wholly: and I pray God your whole spirit, and soul and body, he preserved blameless unto the coming of our Lord Jesus Christ." True Christians are sanctified wholly—in their whole man, though they are not sanctified thoroughly. They are sanctified in every part, though they are not sanctified in the highest degree. Their whole spirit is sanctified, that is, the higher faculties of the soul, namely, the understanding and the will. Their understandings are enlightened by the Spirit unto a spiritual discerning both of good and evil, beyond what any natural man does, or can attain unto. Their wills are bowed, or rather rectified and made straight, being inclined unto God and His law. Their souls are sanctified in the inferior faculties, in all the liking affections—their love, desire, delight, and hope, are towards God, Christ, and things above. Their disliking affections—hatred, fear, grief, and anger, are towards sin. Their bodies also are sanctified, being made members of Christ, and instruments of righteousness; their eyes, ears, tongues, hands, feet, and every part being devoted to God, and made use of for His glory.

Thus, true Christians are sanctified by the Spirit—and they are sanctified unto obedience. The graces which are wrought by the Spirit in their hearts appear in the obedience of their lives; the course of their lives is a course of obedience unto the laws of Christ. They are sanctified unto obedience and they are sanctified unto sprinkling of the blood of Jesus Christ. God has set them apart to be sprinkled with the blood of the immaculate Lamb who takes away sin—that they might be pardoned and saved. Such are true Christians, who love Christ whom they have not seen.

2. Concerning the OBJECT of a true Christian's love, and that is Jesus Christ, whom they have never seen. This Jesus Christ whom they love is the eternal Son of God, the second Person in the glorious Trinity, who in time assumed our human nature, clothed Himself with our mortal flesh, lived like a servant in a poor condition, died like a malefactor the cursed death of the cross—and all for our sakes, for our sins. He rose again the third day for our justification, ascended up into heaven after forty days, and there sat down at the right hand of the throne of the Majesty on high, to make intercession for us, and to make preparation there for our reception into the glorious mansions and eternal habitations which are in the Father's house!

He is called Jesus, from the Hebrew word which signifies "to save," because He saves His people from their sins, Matthew 1:21. He is called Christ, from the Greek, which signifies to anoint, He being anointed by the Father with the Spirit and with power to be Mediator between God and man, to be the great Prophet, and Priest, and King of the Church. This Jesus Christ, Christians in the primitive times, as the Apostles who were of His family and other disciples who conversed with Him frequently, saw Christ with the eye of sense—but it was in His state of humiliation when He was here upon the earth, not in His state of exaltation. Now He is in heaven; yet some have seen Christ after His ascension, namely Paul at his conversion; and Stephen, the first martyr, before he died—but none have had a perfect sight with bodily eyes, of the glory which is upon Christ's body—the luster of which is so great that none can behold it in this state of weakness and imperfection, and live. But whatever sight some Christians have had formerly, no Christians now have a sight of Christ's person. They have heard of Him with the hearing of the ear—but they have not seen Him with the seeing of the eye. They have seen representations of Christ in the Sacrament—but they have never seen His person that is represented. They have seen His image upon their fellow Christians—but they have not seen the original from whom this image has been drawn.

Some Christians have gone to Judea—and seen the place where the Lord lived; and at Jerusalem, and seen the place of His sepulcher, where the Lord, for a time, did lie; and they have seen the mount whence the Lord ascended— but no Christians now alive have been in Jerusalem, and on Mount Zion, which is above, to see where the Lord now is in His glory! It is this Jesus Christ whom Christians have not seen—who is the Object of their love.

3. Concerning the love, which true Christians bear unto this unseen Christ. Love is the going forth of the heart unto the object beloved; and the love which true Christians bear unto Jesus Christ is a grace wrought by the Spirit in their hearts whereby, upon discovery and believing apprehensions of Christ's infinite loveliness and excellency, His matchless love, grace, and mercy—their hearts go forth towards Him in earnest desires after union to Him, and communion with Him, wherein they take chief delight. This is accompanied with a yielding and dedication of themselves unto His will and service.

(1) The love of Christians unto Christ, is a grace wrought in their hearts by the Spirit. Love to Christ is a most sweet and fragrant flower—but there is no seed of this love to Christ, in the nature of any man since the fall. It is planted in the soul by the Spirit of God. Love to Christ is a divine spark which comes down from above; it is a fire

which is kindled by the breath of the Lord, whose essence is love.

(2) The ground of this love to Christ is the discovery and believing apprehensions of Christ's loveliness and love. There must be first a discovery of Christ as a suitable object for love; and not merely a bare notion of this—but believing apprehensions of it, that Christ is infinitely lovely, superlatively excellent, and that His love is matchless and transcended towards His people; that there is a treasure in Him, and a storehouse of all graces, and the most needful and rich supplies. Otherwise there will be no going forth of the heart in love unto Him.

(3) The actings of Christians' love to Christ is in their desires after union unto, and communion with Christ. It is the nature of love, to desire union to the object beloved, especially of this love to Christ; and, this union being attained, the desires are after communion with Christ, converse and fellowship with Him. No converse is so desirable as with those whom we most dearly love; and, this communion being attained, there is chief delight therein. The soul sweetly rests and reposes itself in Christ, and rejoices in His presence and love.

(4) The concomitant of this love which true Christians have unto Christ—is a yielding and dedication of themselves unto His will and service. Lovers give themselves unto those whom they love. This accompanies the marriage union; and such as love Christ are espoused and joined unto Christ, and they give themselves unto Christ to be His and wholly at His disposal, as the wife gives herself unto the disposal of her husband.

4. The fourth thing is—to show that it is the property of all true Christians to love this unseen Christ. True Christians are differenced and distinguished not only from all heathens and infidels—but also from all bare nominal professors, by their love to Jesus Christ. It is the property of covetous people to love worldly wealth and riches. It is the property of ambitious people to love worldly honor and dignities. It is the property of voluptuous people to love sensual pleasures and delights; and it is the property of true Christians to love Jesus Christ, whom they have never seen. None but such as are true Christians, love Christ; and all those who are true Christians love Him. The loveliness of Christ appears not to the eye of sense—but to the eye of faith. Those who do not see Him with this eye, cannot love Him; and those who see Him with this eye cannot but love Him.

Such as do not love Christ, it is not because Christ lacks beauty—but because they are blind! Now all true Christians have this eye of faith to discern Christ's excellencies; and none but true Christians have this eye. The essence of Christianity consists in believing; reason makes us men—but faith makes us true Christians. It being, therefore, the property of true Christians to believe, it is their property also to love this unseen Christ.

5. The fifth thing is—to show that it is the duty of all true Christians to love this unseen Christ. This will appear if you look into John 21:15-17. Peter was one of the boldest and most forward of all Christ's disciples—but he had been too self-confident, which was the introduction unto, and laid the foundation for—his fall and thrice shameful denial of his Master. A look from his Lord put him in remembrance and brought him to repentance with bitter weeping for his sin, as soon as it was committed. After our

Savior was risen from the dead, He appeared unto Peter, with other of His disciples, and in this place asked the same question in the same words three times, "Simon, son of John, do you love Me?" whereby, as He tacitly upbraids him for his great sin in his three-times denial of Him (which, had there not been a defect in his love, he would never have done), so He also gives a signification that love to Himself is the great duty, and the great thing which He looks for, in all His disciples.

6. The sixth thing is—to show HOW Christians ought to love this unseen Christ.

(1) Christians ought to love Christ with SINCERITY of love. Ephesians 6:24, "Grace be with all who love our Lord Jesus Christ in sincerity." It was the great sin of Judah, (Jeremiah 3:10,) that she turned not to the Lord with her whole heart—but insincerely. So it is a great sin to love Christ with an insincere and hypocritical love. The love of Christians to Christ ought to be sincere in regard of the habit and inward workings of it. They must love Him not only in show, word, and outward profession—but their love must be cordial in the heart—and so a love in deed and truth. And the love of Christians to Christ must be sincere in regard of the object of it; they must love Christ for Himself, and not chiefly for what they get by Him. To love Christ only for temporal gain is hypocritical love; to love Christ for His own excellencies and perfections is most sincere and generous. This sincerity of love to Christ, is everyone's duty.

(2) Christians ought to love Christ with SUPREMACY of love. They must place Him in the highest seat of their hearts. He is a great King, and He looks for the throne, and that all creatures should be placed beneath Him

and bow at His footstool, Matthew 10:37, "He who loves father or mother more than Me is not worthy of Me." These are the words of our Savior. Christians may love father and mother, the law of God and nature requires it. They may love husband and wife, the Word of God enjoins the husband to love his wife as his own body, and as Christ loved the church. They may love sons, daughters, brothers, sisters, kindred, friends, yes, enemies—and they ought to do it. Yet all must be with a subordinate love. They must love Christ with their chief love, otherwise they are not worthy to stand in the relation of disciples.

(3) Christians ought to love Christ with ARDENCY of love. Luke 24:32. "Did not our hearts burn within us, while He talked with us by the way, and while He opened to us the Scriptures!" This burning love Christ kindled in the hearts of His disciples; and this burning love, Christ requires of all Christians, Song of Solomon 8:6-7, "For love is as strong as death; ardent love is as unrelenting as the grave. Mighty waters cannot extinguish love; rivers cannot sweep it away." Such a strong, vehement, ardent, flaming love, Christians should have unto Jesus Christ, which all the waters of affliction may not be able to quench, which no floods of temptations or persecutions may be able to drown and overwhelm! Therefore:

(4) Christians ought to love Christ with CONSTANCY of love. Having begun to love Him, they ought to continue to love Him, and to love Him unto the end. As they ought to be constant in their obedience and to persevere in their other graces—so they ought to be constant, and to persevere in this grace of love to Christ.

7. The seventh thing is to show WHY true Christians love Christ, whom they have never seen.

Reason 1. True Christians love Christ—because of the need which they have of Him. Men love their necessary food, without which their bodies would starve with hunger; men love their necessary raiment and habitations, without which, in winter seasons, their bodies would freeze with cold. Men love their necessary friends, upon whom (under God) they have their dependence, and from whom they have all their subsistence. But nothing in the world is as needful to the body—as the Lord Jesus Christ is unto the soul. And, as the excellencies of the soul are far beyond the excellencies of the body, so the necessities of the soul are far beyond the necessities of the body; which necessities can be answered by none but Jesus Christ, and, therefore, true Christians love Him.

At first conversion, when they were convinced of sin and awakened out of their carnal security, O what need had they of Christ! They perceived themselves to be lost, and that it was Christ alone, who could save them! They felt the wounds of conscience, and it was Christ alone, who could heal them! They feared the wrath of a sin-revenging God, and it was Christ alone, who could deliver them! The remission, reconciliation, and salvation, which they had by Christ laid the first foundation of a most endeared love unto Christ; and still they perceive a continual need of Christ to procure daily pardon for them, and to convey daily supplies of grace unto them.

They have need of Christ when they are dark—to enlighten them; when they are dead—to quicken them; when they are straitened—to enlarge them; when they are weak—to strengthen them; when they are sad—to comfort them; when they are tempted—to support them; when they are fallen—to raise them; when they are in doubts—to resolve them; when they are under fears—to encourage them; when they stagger—to establish them; when they wander—to restore them! None but Christ can do all this, and more than this for them. And, therefore, because of the need and usefulness of Christ, true Christians love Him.

Reason 2. True Christians love an unseen Christ—because of the loveliness of Christ; which loveliness, though it is not seen, and cannot here be seen by the eye of the body—yet it is evident unto the eye of faith. See the description which is given of Christ the Beloved by His spouse, the Church, Song of Solomon 5:9. The daughters of Jerusalem there inquire of the love-sick spouse, "What makes the one you love better than another, most beautiful of women? What makes him better than another?" Hereupon the spouse gives a description, verse 10, "My beloved is dark and dazzling, better than ten thousand others!" And after she had set forth His graces, beauties, and excellent accomplishments, in metaphors taken from beauties in the several parts of man's body, in the 11th-14th verses; she concludes, in the 16th verse, "Yes! He is altogether lovely. This is my beloved, and this is my friend!"

The spouse is here acknowledged to be the fairest among women, and not only by the daughters of Jerusalem—but her beloved, who had a more insightful eye, both commends her loveliness and admires it, chapter 6:4-5, "O my beloved, you are as beautiful as the lovely town of Tirzah. Yes, as beautiful as Jerusalem! Look away, for your eyes overcome me!" And, verse 10, "Who is this arising like the dawn, as fair as the moon, as bright as the sun, as majestic as an army with banners?"

But what beauty is there, then, in the Beloved? If the church is beautiful beyond all others, how beautiful is Jesus Christ, from whom the Church derives all its loveliness! He is said to be white and ruddy, that shows the beauty of His face; and His countenance is said to be as Lebanon, and like the lofty cedars thereof, that shows the majesty of His face. His mouth is said to be most sweet; and sweet it is indeed, in regard of the gracious words which proceed from it. No doctrine is so sweet—as Christ's doctrine; no precepts are so sweet—as Christ's precepts; no promises are so sweet—as Christ's promises. But to sum up all excellencies and perfections, in a word, He is said to be "altogether lovely!"

There is no lovely person or thing in the world—which can properly be called "altogether lovely." Many defects may be found in the most amiable people, and much insufficiency may be found in the most desirable things—but Christ is "altogether lovely!" He is unlovely in no respect, there being no spot or blemish, no defect or imperfection, to be found in Him. And He is lovely in every respect; there is an incomparable and transcendent amiableness in Christ's person in every regard. In the person of Christ, the human nature and the divine nature are in conjunction. He is most lovely in regard of both. His human nature is compounded of both body and soul.

His body is most beautiful, a most glorious beauty and luster is put upon it. Whatever it was in His state of humiliation, be sure it has a glorious beauty now in His state of exaltation. It is called a glorious body, Philippians 3:21. If the face of Moses shone with resplendent glory, after his conversing forty days with God in Mount Sinai which was below, how does the body of Christ shine, which has been over seventeen hundred years in Mount

Zion, which is above? I am persuaded that Christ's body is the most beautiful of all visible creatures—but the beauty of Christ's soul excels. No creature whatever has such shining excellencies as are in the soul of Christ. All the excellencies that are, or ever were, in any creature are like a feather laid in the balance with the exceeding weight of His glorious excellencies and perfections!

Christ excelled the most excellent man who ever lived, as to spiritual endowments, when He was here upon earth. He excelled Moses in meekness, Solomon in wisdom, Job in patience; and how much does He excel—now that He is in heaven! He excels not only the spirits of just men made perfect—but also the most glorious and holy angels that never sinned. If any creatures have wisdom, it is but a beam; Christ is the sun! If they have goodness, it is but a drop; in Christ is the ocean! If they have holiness, it is but a spark or dark shadow; Christ is the brightness of His Father's glory! If they have the Spirit, they have it but in some measure; the Spirit is given to Christ without measure! John 3:34.

Christ is most lovely in His manhood, so nearly united unto His Godhead; and how lovely is He in His Godhead! As God, He is equal in all glorious excellencies with the Father. Christ's Godhead implies excellency of being; He calls Himself "I am," John 8:28; excellency of glory, therefore called the "Lord of glory," I Corinthians 2:8; and "King of glory," Psalm 24:7, "Lift up your heads, O you gates; and be you lifted up, you everlasting doors, and the King of glory shall come in." This is interpreted by some to be spoken of Christ's ascension, and the angels and saints making way for His triumphant entrance and possession of His heavenly palace. Many descriptions are given in the New Testament of this lovely person, I shall mention only one, Colossians 1:15-19, "He is the image of the invisible God, the firstborn over all creation. For by him all things were created: things in heaven and on earth, visible and invisible, whether thrones or powers or rulers or authorities; all things were created by him and for him. He is before all things, and in him all things hold together. And he is the head of the body, the church; he is the beginning and the firstborn from among the dead, so that in everything he might have the supremacy. For God was pleased to have all his fullness dwell in him." If we read, believe, and consider this great description of Christ, we must see and say that Christ is most excellent and amiable—and that no beloved is like the beloved of true Christians. Therefore it is, that true Christians love Christ because of His loveliness.

Reason 3. True Christians love Christ—because of His wondrous love, which He bears to them. He loves them with a first love and with a free love. He loves them with a tender and compassionate love, with an active or doing love, with a passive or suffering love. His love is infinite, without bounds of limits. His love is superlative, without comparison. His love is transcendent, beyond comprehension. His love is immutable—without change. His love is eternal—without termination or end. He loved them when they were polluted in their sins, and washed them with His own blood; He loved them when they were naked in their souls, and clothed them with robes of His righteousness. He loves them in their sickness and sorrows, and is their Comforter; He loves them in their needs and straits, and is their Benefactor. He loves them in life, and is the life of their souls; He loves them at death, and is the stay of their hearts; and He loves them after death, and will be their portion forever! "May you experience the love of

Christ, though it is so great you will never fully understand!" Ephesians 3:19

There is great reason that true Christians should love Christ because of His loveliness; and there is further reason that they should love Him because of His love; especially when both are incomparable, both are incomprehensible. I shall further speak (God willing) unto both these with other reasons, under the motives in the exhortation to excite Christians to the love of Christ.

Use 1. For INFORMATION, hence learn that there are but few Christians in deed and in truth. The time has been when openly to profess the name of a Christian argued true love unto Jesus Christ. I mean in the primitive times, when Christians were persecuted by the heathens, as in the ten first dreadful persecutions under the heathen emperors, when the world was watered with Christian blood; then, especially at some times, and in some, yes, most places, whoever openly acknowledged themselves to be Christians exposed themselves unto imprisonments, racks, tortures, burnings, and the most cruel deaths! It was the truth and strength of love unto Jesus Christ—which carried them through such great sufferings as many, in those days, underwent for the sake of Jesus Christ. But now there are multitudes of bare nominal professors. They call themselves Christians, being baptized in Christ's name— but they are altogether without love to Christ, whose name they bear.

Surely there are but few, even in our own land where Christianity is to be found in as great purity as in any place—who love Jesus Christ in sincerity. No grossly ignorant people truly love Christ; such as do not know Christ cannot love Him! There is no desire after, nor love

they have seen; but can you say that you sincerely and chiefly love Jesus Christ, whom you have not seen? The love of the most, arises from the notice which the eye gives of the object beloved; but does your love arise from the notice which the ear has given by the word of the amiableness which there is in Christ?

Question. How may we know whether we have true love to Jesus Christ?

Answer. You may know the truth of your love to Jesus Christ,

first, by your desires after Christ's presence;

second, by your prizing and frequenting those ways wherein Christ is to be found, and seeking Him therein;

third, by your love of Christ's image;

fourth, by your obedience to Christ's commandments.

First, by your desires after Christ's presence. Wherever there is a great love to any person, there is a desire after the presence of that person. Do you sincerely and earnestly desire Christ's presence? There is a twofold presence of Christ: His gracious presence here—and His glorious presence at the last day.

1. There is Christ's GRACIOUS presence here, John 14:18, "I will not leave you comfortless, I will come unto you." You desire that such friends and relations would come unto you—but do you desire chiefly that Christ would come unto you? Christ comes to His disciples in a way of gracious communication, in a way of gracious

manifestation, and in a way of sweet consolation, which results from both.

(1) Do you desire that Christ would come unto you in a way of gracious communication? Are your desires after communication of spiritual light from Christ to teach and guide you; of spiritual life from Christ to quicken and encourage you; of spiritual strength from Christ to support you under burdens, and enable you unto duties? Do you earnestly desire communications of all kinds, and further degrees of grace, out of that fullness of grace which is in Christ? Do you hunger and thirst after Christ's righteousness; not only that it may be imputed to you for your justification—but also that it may be more and more imparted unto you for your further sanctification; that you might be brought, and hereby wrought, into a more perfect conformity and likeness unto Jesus Christ? This is an evidence of true love to Christ.

(2) Do you desire that Christ would come unto you in a way of gracious manifestation? John 14:21, "He who loves Me shall be loved by My Father, and I will love him, and will manifest Myself to him." Do you earnestly desire the fulfilling of this promise so that Christ would reveal to you more of the loveliness of His person and the love of His heart? Are you grieved when your Beloved withdraws Himself; when the curtain is drawn, and a cloud interposes between you and this Sun of righteousness; when He hides and veils His face from you; and do you long after Christ's return and the discoveries of Himself unto you?

"Come, Lord Jesus, come quickly; be as a roe, or a young deer upon the mountains of spices. Leap over the mountains, skip over the hills, and make haste unto my soul, which is love-sick for You in Your absence from me.

O that I might see Your face which is so fair! That I might hear Your voice which is so sweet! That I might feel Your presence which is so refreshing! O that I might behold Your heart-ravishing smiles!"

"Lord, I am Yours and You are mine! You have loved me and given Yourself for me. Your love to me was from everlasting and is unchangeable."

Are these like the breathings of your soul? Such are the breathings of love to Christ.

(3) Do you desire that Christ would come unto you in a way of sweet consolation, which results from this communication and manifestation? Are you desirous after the oil of gladness which Christ is anointed with; that He would give you the unction of the Spirit—not only to sanctify you—but also to comfort you? Do you desire that your hearts may be filled with spiritual joys, the joys of the Holy Spirit, which are unspeakable and full of glory? Do you desire the comforts which Christ gives—beyond all the comforts which the world and the flesh can give; the comforts which come in at the door of faith—beyond all the comforts that come in at the door of sense; those joys which are in Christ—beyond all joys that can be found in the most sweet and desirable creature enjoyment? This evidences true love to Christ. Thus do you desire Christ's gracious presence.

2. And do you desire also Christ's GLORIOUS presence at the last day? When He promises, "Surely I come quickly!" can your hearts make answer, as Revelation 22:20, "Amen, even so, come Lord Jesus!" Are you glad you live so near the end of the world, that the Lord is at hand, and that the coming of the Lord draws nearer and

nearer every day? Can you lift up your heads with joy when you look towards the place where the Lord Jesus Christ is, at the right hand of the throne of the Majesty on high; and think with comfort that yet a little while, and He who shall come, will come, and will not now tarry much longer; that within a short while Christ will descend from heaven with a shout, the Lord with the sound of the trumpet, and that your eyes shall see Him in the brightness of His glory and majesty? Do you look and long for the day of Christ's glorious appearance from heaven, when you shall be awakened out of your graves (where you may take a short sleep before), and be gathered together by the angels and be caught up in the clouds, and there (in shining garments of immortality on your bodies, and of Christ's unspotted righteousness in your souls) be brought with shoutings and acclamations of joy and triumph into His presence, who will then acquit you graciously for all sin and punishment, own you openly for His faithful servants, crown you gloriously before the whole world, and receive you to live and reign with Him to all eternity? Have you such desires as these?

If some of you say you are afraid of Christ's glorious appearance lest then you should be rejected because you fear you are not ready and prepared; yet can you say also from your hearts that you desire above all things that you may be ready; that you endeavor to make ready; that it is your grief that you are no more ready; and that, if you were ready, and were assured of your interest in Christ, you could desire that Christ would come immediately, and that you desire no greater happiness and felicity than to live with Christ in glory; and that you account the presence of Christ in heaven to be the happiness of heaven? These are evidences of true desires after Christ's glorious presence, and of sincere love to Christ.

Secondly, you may know your love to Christ by your prizing and frequenting those ways wherein Christ is to be found, and seeking Him therein. Such are the ways of His ordinances, both public and private. Christ's way is His sanctuary, and in His ordinances He may be found. Do you give your attendance unto ordinances, public prayer, the preaching of the Word, the Lord's Supper; and do you prize these ordinances because of the stamp of Christ's institution upon them, because of Christ's presence in them, and because they are a means of bringing you and Christ together? And, when you are under ordinances—do you diligently seek after Christ in ordinances? Do not you rest in the outside and carnal part of ordinances—in meeting with God's people there? Or do you design, desire, and endeavor after something more inward, spiritual, and incomparably sweet—so that you may meet with Christ there; that you may have fellowship with the Father and the Son there? And, upon this account, can you say as David, "How lovely are Your tabernacles, O Lord! A day in Your courts is better than a thousand!" Psalm 84:10. "One thing have I desired of the Lord, that will I seek after—that I may dwell in the house of the Lord all the days of my life; to behold the beauty of the Lord, and to inquire in His temple!" Psalm 27:4. Do you also seek after Christ in your families and in your closets? Do you seek Him in secret prayer and meditation? Your love to Christ expresses itself in your desires; your desires show themselves in your seeking after Christ in His ways.

Thirdly, you may know your love to Christ by your love of Christ's image. There is the image of Christ on His Word, and there is the image of Christ on His people.

(1) Do you love the image of Christ on His WORD? As Caesar's coin bore Caesar's image and superscription, so

the Word of the Scriptures, which is the Word of Christ, bears Christ's image and superscription. Do you love the Scriptures, because of Christ's image which is upon them? Do You love the Word of doctrine in the Scriptures because of the image of Christ's truth and wisdom upon it? Do you love the Word of precepts in the Scriptures, because of the image of Christ's holiness upon it? Do you love the Word of threatenings in the Scriptures, because of the image of Christ's righteousness upon it? Do you love the Word of promises in the Scriptures, because of the image of Christ's goodness, grace, and love upon it? You have Christ's Word in your Bibles, and sometimes sounding in your ears—but does the Word of Christ dwell in your hearts? You receive Christ's Word in the light of it, do you receive His word in the love of it?

(2) Do you love Christ's image on His PEOPLE? If you do not love your brother whom you have seen, how can you love your Lord whom you have not seen? All of Christ's disciples bear Christ's image; if you love the original you will love the picture, although it is but imperfectly drawn. If you love the perfect goodness and holiness which is in Christ—you will love the goodness and holiness which you see in the saints, although they have it but in an imperfect measure. Do you love Christ's disciples, and that because of Christ's image, although they differ from you in some secondary matters?

Fourthly, you may know your love to Christ by your obedience unto His commandments. John 14:15, 21, "If you love Me, keep My commandments. He who has My commandments, and keeps them, he it is who loves Me." You have Christ's commandments—do you keep them? You know them, do you practice them? Your love to Christ—is known by your obedience unto Christ. If Christ is your beloved—He is also your Lord; if you have true affection for Him—you will yield subjection unto Him. If you love Christ, you are careful to please Christ; you are not the servants of the flesh, to take care to please the flesh—but you are the servants of Christ to take care above all people and all things—to please Christ.

If you love Christ, you are fearful of giving just occasion of offense unto men but, above all, you are fearful of displeasing and offending your Lord. Do you labor so to walk that you may please Christ in the way of sincere and universal obedience? Are you hearty in your obedience unto Christ? Have you a respect to all His commandments? Is it your grief—that you fall short in your obedience unto Christ? If you can say in the presence of the Lord and your hearts (do not give your tongues the lie) that you do not live and allow yourselves in the practice of any known sin which Christ forbids, nor in the neglect of any known duty which Christ commands—this is a sure evidence of true love to Jesus Christ. Thus for the trial of your love unto Christ.

Use 3. For REPROOF.

First, to all such as have NO love at all unto this unseen Christ. And will not the use of information, together with the use of trial, leave a conviction upon many of you, that you are without this love? Allow, then, the word of reproof. What! Are you creatures made by Christ, and made for Christ—and yet have no love to Him? Are you rational creatures? Do you have souls capable of knowing Him and loving Him, and yet have no love? Are some of you professors, and yet do not love Christ? Do you make a show of devotion—and yet are without any true affection to the object of your worship? Sinners, have you not heard enough to engage and draw forth your love unto Christ? What do you think? Is there such a person as Jesus Christ—or is there not? Have you no Bibles? And, if you have, have you not read therein the history concerning Jesus Christ? And what do you think of that history? Is it true or false? Do you think that the gospel is a cunningly devised fable? Are not the Scriptures, which contain this gospel, the very Word of the true God—who cannot lie? Are there not such characters of divinity upon them as are sufficient to evidence their divine origin to any who search into them and do not willfully shut their eyes against the light which there shines? And, if it is so that there is indeed such a person as Jesus Christ (as there is nothing more true), how is it that you have no love unto Him? Do not the Scriptures reveal and set forth Christ as the most excellent and amiable Person—and yet do you not love Him? Can you love people and things that are but imperfectly lovely—and not love Jesus Christ who is altogether lovely!

Can you love one who has some inferior honor and power and authority—and not love Jesus Christ who is the Lord of glory, who has all power and authority both in heaven and earth? Can you love such as have some earthly wisdom and learning—and not love Jesus Christ, who is the wisdom of the Father, who knows all things, and whose wisdom is divine? Can you love such as are somewhat liberal and bountiful—and not love Christ, whose bounty is superlative, and whose gifts are most rich and transcendent? Can you love friends who are somewhat kind—and not love Jesus Christ, who is the best friend that men ever had? Can you love a benefactor who feeds you, and clothes you, and gives money to you—and yet not love Christ, who offers to feed your hunger-starved souls with the Bread of Life, to clothe your naked souls with the robes of His righteousness, and to give the spiritual riches of grace to you, the least of which is of more worth than all the riches of the earth?

Can you love riches—and not love Christ, in whom there are treasures, and by whom you may have not only spiritual riches here—but also the heavenly inheritance hereafter? Can you love honors—and not love Christ, by whom you may have the highest dignities, the honor of children to the King of heaven now, and a crown of glory in the heavenly world? Can you love liberty—and not love Christ, by whom you may be made free from the slavery of the devil and your own lusts? Can you love safety—and not love Christ, who is the only Savior of mankind, and who alone puts you in safety from the reach of the worst of enemies, and worst of evils? Can you love peace—and not love Christ, by whom you may have peace with God and peace in your own conscience? Can you love pleasures and delights—and not love Christ, by whom you may have joys unspeakable and full of glory, besides those everlasting pleasures which are to come?

Without love to Christ, you are under the guilt of all your sins; neither your original sin, nor any of your actual sins are pardoned. They all lie upon your own score, and you must answer for all yourselves, and how fearful is your account likely to be!

Without love to Christ, you are under the curse; not only under the curse of the law for your breach of the law—but also under the curse of the gospel, for disobedience to this command of the gospel, which requires you to love the Lord Jesus Christ, 1 Corinthians 16:22, "If anyone does not love the Lord, that person is cursed! Come, O Lord!" That is, let him be cursed until the Lord comes. And, when the Lord comes, will He take off the curse from you? No! He will come in flaming fire, to take vengeance upon you, having threatened then to punish all such with everlasting destruction as shall be found to have disobeyed the gospel. And what will become of you? Sodom and Gomorrah, those wicked cities, will then be punished dreadfully with a worse fire than that which was rained down from heaven, and consumed their people and habitations together; I mean, with the fire of hell which will be kindled and kept alive unto eternity by the breath of the Almighty!

But you who do not love the Lord Jesus Christ, notwithstanding all discoveries of Him, invitations to Him, and offers of kindnesses by Him—you will be punished more dreadfully than the wicked Sodomites! It will be more tolerable in the day of judgment for them—than for you. The torments of hell will be intolerable for any—but they will be most intolerable for gospel sinners; the fire of hell will burn upon you the most fiercely, and the scourge of conscience will lash you the most furiously! Consider this, all you who have no love to Christ; otherwise, when He comes to judgment, He will tear you to pieces and there will be none to deliver you! If you do not have the sweet fire of love to Christ kindled in your hearts here—you will be thrown into the dreadful fire of hell which will burn you everlastingly!

Second, this reproves such of you as have SOME love—but it is very little love to Jesus Christ. You who love Christ—is not your love very small not only in comparison with His love to you—but also in comparison with the love which some Christians have attained unto? How strong was the love of the Apostles unto Christ— when they left all and followed Him, especially after the resurrection of Christ and His ascension into heaven. O what a fire of love unto Christ was then enkindled within them! Hence, that bold profession which they make of Christ before the chief priests and elders, Acts 4. Hence their rejoicing that they were counted worthy to suffer shame for the name of Christ, when they were beaten for their owning and preaching of Him, Acts 5:41.

The love of Peter and John was great unto Christ, and the love of Paul was not inferior unto the love of the chief Apostles; hence it was that he took such pains to preach the gospel in so many parts of the world, Romans 15:19. See, also, how he approves himself to be a minister of Christ, and gives evidences of his strong love to his Master, 2 Corinthians 11:23-29, "I have served him far more! I have worked harder, been put in jail more often, been whipped times without number, and faced death again and again. Five different times the Jews gave me thirty-nine lashes. Three times I was beaten with rods. Once I was stoned. Three times I was shipwrecked. Once I spent a whole night and a day adrift at sea. I have traveled many weary miles. I have faced danger from flooded rivers and from robbers. I have faced danger from my own people, the Jews, as well as from the Gentiles. I have faced danger in the cities, in the deserts, and on the stormy seas. And I have faced danger from men who claim to be Christians but are not. I have lived with weariness and pain and sleepless nights. Often I have been hungry and thirsty and have gone without food. Often I have shivered with cold, without enough clothing to keep me warm. Then, besides all this, I have the daily burden of how the churches are getting along." 2 Corinthians 11:23-29

And, chapter 12:10, "I delight in weaknesses, in insults, in hardships, in persecutions, in difficulties, for Christ's sake." The ground of all of this was the love of

Christ which constrained him, 2 Corinthians 5:14. He had such a love to Christ that he professed, Philippians 1:21, "To me to live is Christ, and to die is gain!" Christ was his life, and his life was wholly at Christ's devotion.

But where is such love now to be found? I might speak also of the love of some ancient fathers, Ignatius, Polycarp. Jerome, and others. Take one instance in Jerome who thus expressed his love unto Christ, "If my father were weeping on his knees before me, my mother hanging on my neck behind me, my brethren, sisters, and kinsfolk howling on every side, to retain me in a sinful course—I would fling my mother to the ground, run over my father, despise all my kindred, and tread them under my feet, that I might run unto Christ!"

How little is your love in comparison with the love of those famous heroes, I mean those eminent martyrs, who have despised the flames and endured such racking and torturing deaths for the love which they bore unto Jesus Christ; the fire of their love burning stronger within them— than the fire without them in which their bodies were consumed! Is not your love also small in comparison with the love of our late reformers, which fired them with such courage and resolution as to withstand a whole world of anti-Christian fury and opposition? Is your love comparable to that of many eminent divines and private Christians of our own nation, of the age immediately going before, who are now asleep in their graves; but how few are there come up in their place?

It is observed, and it is greatly to be lamented, that there is, of late years, a great decay in the power of godliness among those who are sincere; and is it not evident in the great decay of love, even in true Christians, unto Jesus Christ? Are not you dwarfs in comparison with others? Are not you babes in Christ, and weaklings in your love to Christ? Is it not evident that you have but little love to Christ—when He is but little in your thoughts and meditations? The thoughts are the handmaids of love. Where the love is strong and ardent, there many thoughts will be attending upon it; but will not your hearts tell you that your thoughts of Christ are very few? You can think often of your food—but how little do your thoughts feed upon Christ, who is the Bread of Life? You can often think of your raiment—but how little do you think of the robes of Christ's righteousness? You can think often of your earthly friends—but how little do you think of Jesus Christ, your friend in heaven?

Objects of sense are often not only in your eyes—but also in your thoughts—but how little is Christ entertained in your thoughts, who is the object of faith? Moreover, does it not argue little love to Christ, that you speak so little of Him and for Him in your conversing one with another? If you had much love to Christ—would not this love breathe forth more in your discourses?

You can readily speak of yourselves, and do often, either directly or indirectly, commend yourselves, which reveals your great self-love. How little do you commend your Lord and Master, and extol His excellencies with your lips! And does not this evidence that you have but little love to Him in your hearts? You can readily discourse of news and public occurrences (which is lawful and needful)—but when you leave Christ quite out of your discourse, it shows that you have not an abundance of love to Him because, out of the abundance of the heart, the mouth will speak of their riches. Such as have much love to pleasures will be often speaking of that subject, such as love their friends much will be often speaking and commending them when they are in company. And when you speak but little of Christ, it is a sign that you love Him but little.

Does not the little zeal which you have for Christ's honor in the world argue that you have but little love to Him? Where is your activity for Christ to promote His interest among those relations and friends that you have acquaintance with? Do you labor all you can—to bring others into the ways of God and into acquaintance with Christ? Besides, will not your little secret devotion, argue your little affection unto Christ? Will not your closets, or other retiring places, witness how little you are in secret prayer and converse with Christ there? Brief and straitened prayer in secret, argues a heart straitened in love to Jesus Christ.

Does not your backwardness to the exercise of this love to Christ, show the weakness of your love? How slow of heart are you to the love of Christ! How hard to be persuaded! You need not be persuaded to love your wives, if they are kind and helpful; you need not be persuaded to love your children, if they are kind and hopeful; you need not be persuaded to love your friends, if they are friendly and faithful; and yet, whatever attractions of love, the most strong of any—are in Jesus Christ! You are backward to this love.

Need I say more to convince you that you have but little love to Christ? Will not your own conscience, from these clear evidences, sufficiently witness the thing? And now, Christians, think what a sin, what a shame, what a folly it is—that you should have so little love unto Jesus Christ! If it is so great a sin for such as are strangers unto

Christ, to have no love at all to Him, so that it brings them under the most dreadful curse, surely it cannot be a small sin that you (who are His true disciples) should have but little love unto Him! Is it not very displeasing to the Father that you should have but little love to His Son? If He does not hate you because of your relation unto Christ—yet is He not angry with you for the lukewarmness of your affection unto Christ, which sin is aggravated by the nearness of your relation?

Is it not dishonorable unto Christ—that you should have so little love to Him? Do you not, in effect, say there is no great worth or amiableness in Him—when you have no great love unto Him? Are you not hereby ungrateful unto Christ beyond what can be paralleled by any ingratitude unto the most obliging earthly friend? Is it not your shame that you should have so little love to Christ—when He so much deserves your love? Besides the infinite excellencies and perfections which are in Him—does not His infinite kindness unto you, call for both the truth and the strength of your love?

Think what He has done for you; think what He has suffered for you. Think what He has purchased for you; think what He has promised to you. Think what He has laid out for you; think what He has laid up for you—and yet to have but little love to Christ! Yet to make such poor returns!

Moreover, is it not your folly to have but little love to Christ? Do not you hereby bereave yourselves, or debar yourselves of such a peace as passes all understanding, of such sweetness and comfort both in the strength of your love—and in the sense of His love as is inconceivable? Is not injury and harm unto yourselves, the consequence of your little love unto Christ? Must you not draw on so heavily in the ways of God, as Pharaoh when his chariot-wheels were taken off? Love to Christ is like wheels in your motion for Christ, and like oil to the wheels which makes you ready unto any good work which He calls you unto! But when you have but little love unto Christ, you must be more slow in your motions, more sluggish in Christ's service. You will not, you cannot, take those pains in the work of the Lord and be as zealous as you might, and should be, for your Master's glory.

To conclude, if you have but little love to Christ—you will be apt to faint in the day of adversity, to shrink when you are called to take up His cross and suffer for His sake. Lesser sufferings will discompose you, greater sufferings will frighten and amaze you, and you will be in danger of turning into fearful apostates in time of great trials. There is need of great love to Christ, as well as great faith—to carry you through sufferings with courage, that you may persevere unto the end.

Use 4. For exhortation unto the love of Jesus Christ, whom you have never seen; this is the use chiefly designed in the choice of this subject, and which I shall most largely insist upon. In the prosecution of it, I shall give some motives and then some directions.

The motives to induce and excite you unto the love of this unseen Christ, may be drawn—

(1) from the consideration of what Christ is;

(2) from the consideration of Christ's love;

(3) froth the consideration of Christ's benefits;

(4) from the consideration of that love which Christians have, and should have, unto Christ.

The first sort of motives, may be drawn from the consideration of what Christ is:

(1) what He is in Himself;

(2) what He is to the Father;

(3) what He is unto true Christians.

First, consider what Christ is in HIMSELF. In general, He is the most amiable Person and the most suitable Object for your love. If you ask of the days which are past, since the day that God created man upon the earth; if you seek from one side of heaven unto the other; if you make inquiry into all the parts of the earth—you will never find that there never was, or is to be found—any person so lovely, so beautiful, and so every way deserving your love—as the Lord Jesus Christ. There is a matchless, transcendent, and incomparable beauty and excellency in Him!

How passionately are some foolish men in love with the external beauty which they see in some women! They love the exact symmetry of parts, and lovely proportion of the body—the amiable features and lovely mixtures of colors in the face—the beauty of the eyes and features, their graceful motions, and amorous glances. How does this ravish the hearts of some foolish men, although the most beautiful woman in the world is no better than a mixture of clay, dirt, and corruption enclosed in a lovely skin, which sickness will cause to look pale and wane—and death will fully mar and spoil! But the amiableness and beauty of

Christ is more transcendent and permanent, and therefore, a more fit object for your love. Christ is fairer than the children of men. He is all fair—without any spot; altogether lovely—without any blemish or deformity!

I have already spoken of the glorious beauty which is in Christ's glorified body—the most lovely of any visible creature which God has made; and also of the shining excellencies which are in Christ's glorified soul—so nearly joined to the divinity. Could we suppose all the loveliness that ever was seen or found in the most lovely people that ever lived, were to meet in one person—how lovely would that person be? Yet such, though ever so resplendent beauty—would be but a dark shadow compared with the brightness of our most beautiful Christ! Can you love the imperfect beauty which you see in creatures, and will you not love the perfect beauty which there is in Christ! Can you love a fading beauty which soon withers like the flower—and will you not love Christ—whose beauty never decays—but always abides more fresh than beauty in the flower of youth! Can you be soon affected with beautiful objects which are before the eye of your sense, and will you not be affected with this far more beautiful object, the Lord Jesus Christ—who is so clearly discernible by the eye of faith? If the eye of your faith was open and clear, to look upon the transcendent loveliness which is in Christ—you could not but love Him! Could you see the glances of His eye, and the sweet smiles of His lovely face—your hearts would be overcome and ravished with love, and filled with ecstasies of joy and ineffable delight! "Yes! He is altogether lovely! This is my Beloved, this my Friend!" Song of Songs 5:16

More particularly, there are the most amiable qualifications in Christ's person, to attract and draw forth your love. I shall instance in these six:

(1) His greatness and authority;

(2) His holiness and purity;

(3) His wisdom and omniscience;

(4) His truth and faithfulness;

(5) His fullness and all sufficiency;

(6) His kindness and mercy.

1. Consider Christ's GREATNESS and AUTHORITY. The eagle does not pursue after flies. Great souls are not affected, unless it is with great things. There is none so great as Jesus Christ! He is most great in honor and dignity; He is most great in power and authority.

Excellency of majesty greatly engages the love, and commands the hearts, as well as the obedience of subjects. Those princes that have the greatest power and authority, when they do not abuse their place by unrighteousness and cruelty, by usurpation and tyranny—are the darlings of the people. If power is managed with mercifulness, and authority with kindness, towards those who are under command—so highly do princes advance themselves hereby in the esteem and love of their people, that they will be ready to spend their estates, and venture their lives, in their service!

Christ is the Prince of the kings of the earth. He is clothed with the highest honor, arrayed with the most excellent majesty, decked with the largest power, and invested with the greatest authority. He is the King and Lord of glory! He is exalted to higher dignity than the greatest potentate that ever lived upon the earth! Yes, He is advanced above all thrones and dominions, principalities and powers, of the glorious angels that are in heaven! All power is given to him in heaven and earth, Matthew 28:18. He does what He will in heaven—the angels are at His beck and execute His will, go and come at His command. And He has power on earth. He is the Head of the church, and Head over all unto the church. He can restrain His enemies, and conquer them, and bring them under His feet at His pleasure. And whatever severity He shows sometimes in executing His judgments and taking vengeance on the wicked—He never abuses His power by unrighteousness. He is most just towards the worst, and punishes them less that their iniquities deserve. But what kindness and mercifulness does He show to His own subjects and people; and will not you have a great love—to so great a person! Should not the consideration of the high dignity of your Lord raise your love of Him unto a great height? When Christ has such authority, shall He not command your hearts? When Christ is invested with such power that He can defend you against the rage and cruelty of your most powerful and malicious adversaries, will not you greatly love such a magnanimous person, as well as confidently trust under the shadow of His government?

2. Consider Christ's HOLINESS and PURITY. Some great people who abound in wealth and honor, who have some kind of amiable natural qualities, and acquired accomplishments which might render them very useful in their countries—yet through their wickedness and

debauchery, their filthiness and impurity, their impious and wicked lives—they stain all other excellencies and render themselves the objects of contempt and scorn—unto those who, otherwise, would bear great respect and love to them.

But Christ is most amiable for His holiness and purity. He was holy in His birth; although born of a sinful woman—yet He was born without sin. When He lived among impure sinners—He kept His garments from all stains and spots. His heart and life were free from all pollutions, and never was He guilty of the least transgression, either in action or the least inclination. O what an excellent person was Christ when here upon the earth! How glorious in holiness! What bright beams of perfect purity and spotless innocency, did Christ scatter in those dark places of the earth where He lived, and among those dark and sullied sinners with whom He conversed! How, then, does Christ shine in holiness—now that He is entered into the Holy of Holies which is above, and there converses with none but such as are holy!

Because of Christ's holiness and purity—He is now the object of the hatred and enmity of the wicked and ungodly. Because Christ is an enemy unto their darling and beloved lusts—they have an enmity against the holiness of Christ. When He was here below, He told His brethren, John 7:7, "The world hates Me—because I testify that what it does is evil!" And the hatred of the world to Christ, still abides upon the same account.

Christ reproves the world of sin—and this the world cannot endure. The bright beams of Christ's holiness—wound their sore eyes! His holy precepts offend their carnal hearts! Yet, notwithstanding this, He is a most suitable object for the love of saints—upon the account of His holiness. Such as are truly judicious, will love them most, who are best; and such are really the best men and women in the world as are most holy. If you are Christ's disciples indeed, you love holiness wherever you see it; and can you love the imperfect holiness which is in God's people, and will you not love Christ who is perfectly, infinitely holy Himself, and the spring of all that holiness which is to be found in any of the children of men? If there is such a wonderful luster in the derived holiness of some, that it makes them to shine as lights in a dark world—what a wonderful transcendent luster is there in the original holiness which is in Christ! Which, as it is a matter of great admiration, so it calls for great affection, Psalm 119:140, "Your Word is very pure, therefore Your servant loves it." Christ is the Word; not the written Word—but the essential Word: and He is very pure. Therefore you should love Him!

3. Consider Christ's WISDOM and OMNISCIENCE. Wisdom makes the face to shine. Learning advances some very highly in esteem; such as know most, if their morals are suitable to their intellects—are most admired by those who understand what true worth is, especially if there is spiritual wisdom in conjunction with natural and acquired knowledge. If there is such grace in the heart, as well as much knowledge in the head—how worthy are such to be loved?

Daniel was a man of great learning and wisdom, skilled in all the learning of the Chaldeans which was not sinful and diabolical; and besides this, He was endowed with divine wisdom by the teachings of the Holy Spirit. The angel told this Daniel—that he was a man greatly beloved. He was greatly beloved by his king, and greatly beloved by his people, and by all—except some few who

envied his prosperity and favor. If Daniel's wisdom
rendered him so universally amiable, how then should
Christ be loved—because of His wisdom and knowledge?
The wisdom of Christ is far beyond the wisdom of Daniel,
or the wisdom of Solomon, who was wiser than Daniel.
These men had wisdom which made them famous and
esteemed in their day—but Christ is wisdom itself—the
wisdom of the Father. They were children of wisdom—but
Christ is the Father and fountain of wisdom. They had
some particles of wisdom—but the treasures of wisdom are
hid and laid up in Christ! Colossians 2:3.

They had learning and knowledge—but their
knowledge was ignorance, when compared with the
knowledge of Christ. They knew some things—but Christ
is omniscient and knows all things; they knew many secrets
of nature—but Christ knows the secrets of heaven, the
mind of God—and nothing is hidden from Him. How
greatly beloved, then, should Christ be! If you are wise—
you will love Christ; if you would be wise—you must love
Christ, who is so infinitely wise Himself, and who alone
can make you truly wise!

4. Consider Christ's TRUTH and FAITHFULNESS.
Truth and faithfulness are very rare in our day, when
falsehood and deceit so much abound. What was said of
old, Isaiah 59:14, "truth fails and falls in the street," the
same may be said now; and, therefore, such as are faithful
and without deceit, are worthy of great esteem and love.
But what love should you give unto Christ—who is not
only true—but truth itself; who is most faithful in all His
undertakings and promises, and never deceived any who
put their trust in Him—who is often better than His Word!
You will love a true and faithful friend—and will you not
love a true and faithful Christ, the best friend of men? As

Christ's faithfulness should encourage your confidence in
Him—so it should endear your love unto Him.

5. Consider Christ's FULLNESS and ALL-
SUFFICIENCY. Such as have large and plentiful estates
are greatly loved by the poor and indigent—if they find
them also to have large hearts and open hands, ready to
distribute unto their needs and necessities. None have such
fullness and plenty as the Lord Jesus Christ—and none are
so willing to give of His fullness unto the needs of such as
are poor in spirit, and sensible of their need, Colossians
1:19, "It has pleased the Father, that in Him all fullness
should dwell!" There is not only fullness in Him—but all
fullness; not the fullness of the cistern—but the fullness of
the fountain; not the fullness only of sufficiency for
Himself—but the fullness of redundancy for His people;
not some fullness for some things—but all fullness for all
things that are good; not fullness for some time, and to
continue but for awhile—but all fullness dwells in Him,
and abides for all His people throughout all generations.
And this not to depend on the pleasure of men, whose
minds may alter—but it has pleased the Father, and
depends upon the pleasure of the Father, who is always the
same, and whose good-will to His people is unchangeable.

There is a twofold fullness in Christ for His people
here on earth, besides His fullness of glory, which has a
reference to eternity. There is a fullness of merit, and a
fullness of spirit:

(1) There is a fullness of merit, in that full and perfect
righteousness which He has wrought out for them, and
which He imputes unto them for their justification.

(2) There is a fullness of Spirit in Christ, the Spirit being given unto Him without measure, which He imparts and communicates unto them for their sanctification and consolation.

Christians, you are empty—Christ is full! You are poor—Christ is rich! You are indigent—Christ is all-sufficient! Will not you love Christ, who is able to do for you beyond what you are able to ask or think, and is as willing as He is able to supply all your spiritual necessities? Will you not love Christ, who is an overflowing and everflowing fountain of goodness; who has inexhaustible treasures of graces and comforts in Him, which are set open before you, and unto you—and every day you may freely come and fetch such jewels out of this treasury as are of higher worth, greater use, than any earthly riches, in the greatest plenty and abundance?

6. Consider Christ's KINDNESS and MERCY. All the kindness of men—is unkindness, when compared with the kindness of Christ! All the mercies of men—are cruelty, when compared with the mercies of Christ. He is all kindness, all affection, all compassion, all pity, all grace, all mercy—to miserable lost mankind. I shall not enlarge here, because this will fall under the second head of arguments taken from the consideration of Christ's love. If you add the kindness and mercy of Christ, to all His other excellencies and perfections, surely He will appear to have incomparable the greatest attractions in Him for love, unto any who have not a very thick veil of unbelief before their eyes, to hide Him from their view!

Secondly, consider what Christ is to the FATHER:

(1) He is most nearly related to Him.

(2) He is most dearly beloved by Him.

(1) Christ is most nearly RELATED, and most perfectly LIKE, unto the Father. All the creatures are related to God as their Maker—but God's children are more nearly related. The saints are nearly related to God, who are His children by adoption and regeneration. The angels are more nearly related to God, who are His sons by creation and never were separated from Him by sin. But the Lord Jesus Christ is most nearly related unto God, who is His Son by eternal generation. Thus, Christ is the only begotten Son of God, and bears His image most perfectly, being the brightness of His Father's glory, and the express image of His person. This near relation of Christ, and His likeness to the Father, calls for your strongest love.

You have reason to love the Son. You will love the sons of princes, and will you not love the Son of God? You will love your own children who bear your own image, and will you not love Christ, who is the express image of God? We read of Christ, Philippians 2:6, "Who, being in the form of God, thought it not robbery, to be equal with God." Christ (without robbery or derogation unto God) is equal with God in all glorious excellencies and perfections and, therefore, your highest and strongest love is His due; and, without robbery, you cannot withhold it from Him.

(2) Christ is most dearly BELOVED by the Father. 2 Peter 1:17, "For He received from God the Father honor and glory, when there came such a voice to Him from the excellent glory—This is my beloved Son, in whom I am well pleased." He, then, who is worthy of the Father's love, surely is worthy of yours; He who is chiefly beloved by the Father—should chiefly be beloved by you.

Thirdly, consider what Christ is unto all true CHRISTIANS. If you are a true believer, Christ is your Shepherd. He feeds you in green pastures; He has laid down His life for His sheep—and will you not love such a Shepherd?

Christ is your Captain who has conquered all your enemies for you, and leads you on to take the spoils—and will you not love such a Leader?

Christ is your Prophet who teaches you the most excellent things that ever were taught, the highest mysteries, the most glorious truths, which are of the greatest concern to know and believe; and He teaches you in the most excellent way by His Word and Spirit; opening your understandings as well as His truths, giving you light and an eye to discern this light—and will you not love such a Teacher?

Christ is your High Priest who has made an atoning sacrifice for your sins to reconcile you unto God. He now makes intercession for you—which is incessant and prevalent. Will you not love such an Advocate?

Christ is your King, who rules you most powerfully and righteously, most wisely and graciously—and will you not love such a Sovereign?

Christ is your Benefactor, the most kind and bountiful, and no gifts are comparable unto His gifts—and will you not love such a Friend?

Christ is your Brother, and, if He is not ashamed to own you for His brothers and sisters, will it not be a shame if you should withhold from Him your hearts?

Christ is your Husband, and you are joined to Him by the Spirit and faith in such bonds as cannot be broken—and will not you embrace Him in the arms of your dearest love?

Christ is your Redeemer, who rescued and delivered you from sin and Satan, from death and wrath! He has redeemed you by price, the price of His blood. Has He not, then, given the greatest price for your love? He has redeemed you also by conquest, and shall He not make a conquest of your hearts?

Surely you are altogether unworthy of these relations if you do not present Christ with your most endeared and choicest affections.

Thus far the motives drawn from the consideration of what Christ is.

The second sort of motives to excite your love to Christ, may be drawn from the consideration of Christ's love unto true Christians. If you are Christians indeed, Christ loves you:

(1) with the freest love;
(2) with the truest love;
(3) with the strongest love;

(4) with the surest love.

1. Consider that Christ loves you with the FREEST love. "We love Him—because He first loved us." 1 John 4:19. There are many motives and attractions for your love to Christ—but Christ's love to you is most free. There is nothing in yourselves to draw and engage His love—except your deformity and enmity to Him, except filthiness which

He loathes, and wickedness which His soul hates; these are
the only motives. There is no man in the world who loves
you, but he finds or fancies some loveliness in you,
something to be a motive to draw his love to you. Wit is a
motive to some, wealth to others, beauty to some, strength
to others, near relation to some, dear love to others,
liberality to some, service to others, greatness to some,
goodness to others. Likeness, whether it is in good or evil,
is a motive to the love of the most. But Christ's first love to
you is altogether free; that which is a motive to men, and
induces their love to you, is no motive to incline the love of
Christ.

The sin which you brought into the world with you,
and the many sins which, since you came into the world,
have been committed by you, are enough to shut out all
motives of love in Christ, unto whom all sin is so odious
and abominable. Whatever motive induces Christ to love
you, it was not drawn from yourselves—but it was drawn
from His own affectionate heart! Will not this free love of
Christ to you--incline you to love Him? Does He love you
most freely, and will you not love Him most dearly? Did
Christ love you without any motive to draw His love, and
will you not love Christ, in whom there are so many
motives to draw your love? Did Christ begin to love, and
will not you make a return? Did Christ love you with all
your sinfulness and vileness, and will you not love Him in
whom there is such perfect beauty? If you now have any
spiritual beauty, it is through the loveliness which Christ
has put upon you! Christ's free and sovereign love—is a
matter of the greatest admiration, and should be a motive
unto the greatest affection unto Him.

2. Consider that Christ loves you with the TRUEST
love. There is little true love in the world. You have many

who truly hate you—but few who truly love you. Also, there is much deception in the pretended love and affection of some. All who flatter you—do not truly love you. Love in show and outward appearance, in good words and fair speeches, is common. But love in deed and in truth evidences itself in real offices of love. Where there is the greatest need, this true love is rarely to be found. Job complains, in Job 6:15-17. "My brothers have proved as unreliable as a seasonal brook that overflows its banks in the spring when it is swollen with ice and melting snow. But when the hot weather arrives, the water disappears. The brook vanishes in the heat." In the prosperity of Job, he had many friends, and their love and friendship seemed to have some strength and consistency like the ice upon the brook; but when heat of trouble and calamity came upon Job, then the love of his friends melted and vanished away like ice and snow, before the warm beams of the sun. The love of most is selfish, for their own ends and, therefore, when their love is not likely to be beneficial to them—but rather create trouble to themselves, it comes to nothing.

True Christianity teaches another kind of love, and those who are really pious have a true love, which is ready to show itself most in an adverse state. But none do or can love you with such a true love as Jesus Christ; there is no flattery or deception in His love. His love is not in the least counterfeit, it is not in the least selfish and for His own ends. He does not love you to receive good from you—but that He might do good unto you. He loves you not only in prosperity—but chiefly He evidences His love in affliction and adversity. He is a present help in the time of trouble, and then gives the most tender demonstrations of His love. He is touched with the feelings of your infirmities when you are tempted, and sympathizes with you in your sorrows when you are afflicted. He shows His love in visiting you under your troubles, in supporting you, in relieving you, and in delivering you. Oh! What love should you have unto the Lord Jesus Christ, who loves you with such a true and sincere love!

3. Consider that Christ loves you with the STRONGEST love. His love is stronger than death, more ardent than fire which has a most vehement flame. The strength of Christ's love to you shows itself in the activity of His love, in His doing for you; and this will appear in three things:

(1) in what He has done for you;

(2) in what He is doing for you;

(3) in what He will do for you.

(1) The strength and activity of Christ's love to you shows itself in what Christ HAS done for you. I shall briefly name some particulars:

It was the strong love of Christ which brought Him down from heaven for you, to assume your nature. What kind of love was this—that God should become man! That spirit should become flesh, that He who made the world should be born of a poor virgin, and all for your sakes!

It was the love of Christ which made Him to fulfill all righteousness for you. He yielded perfect obedience to the law, both moral and ceremonial, that you might have the benefit of it.

It was the love of Christ which made Him submit Himself to the temptations of the devil for you—so that He, suffering, being tempted, might be able to support you when you are tempted.

It was the love of Christ which made Him endure the contradictions of sinners for you. He bore many affronts, abuses, envyings, and blasphemies of wicked men—that He might give you an example how to carry yourselves under similar circumstances.

It was the love of Christ which made Him lay down His life for you; John 15:13-14, "Greater love has no man than this, that a man lay down his life for his friends. You are My friends!" That such a person as Christ, so excellent, so innocent—should undergo death, and such a death as that of the cross—so disgraceful, so painful; that He should submit to such ignominy, and endure such agony, such tearing in the flesh, such pressures in His spirit; and that with such resolution and willingness, with such submission and patience; and that for such as you, although now His friends—yet, while in a state of nature, you were His strangers and enemies; here was love stronger than death! Oh, the height, oh the depth of this love! There are such dimensions in this love of Christ, as the longest line of your most extended thoughts and imaginations, can never be able to reach and measure.

It was the love of Christ which raised Him again from the dead for you; Romans 4:25, "Who was delivered for your offences, and was raised again for our justification."

It was the love of Christ which carried Him up from earth to heaven, where He was before you, John 16:7 "It is for your benefit that I go away, because if I don't go away, the Comforter will not come to you. If I go, I will send Him to you."

(2) The strength and activity of Christ's love to you—
shows itself in what He IS doing for you.

He is interceding for you at the right hand of God,
Romans 8:34, "Who is he that condemns? Christ Jesus,
who died—more than that, who was raised to life--is at the
right hand of God and is also interceding for us." It is
through love, that Christ pleads for you in heaven that you
may be accepted, your sins pardoned, your prayers
answered, and the Holy Spirit may be sent down to you to
teach, sanctify, and comfort you.

He is preparing a place for you, John 14:2, "In My
Father's house are many dwelling places; if not, I would
have told you. I am going away to prepare a place for you."
It is through love that Christ, as your forerunner, has for
you entered into the glorious palace which is above, to take
possession of it for you, and to prepare places there for
your reception.

(3) The strength and activity of Christ's love to you—
shows itself in what He WILL do for you.

He will keep you in His hand so that none shall pluck
you thence, John 10:28, "They shall never perish, neither
shall any pluck them out of My hand!" Because you are
received into the arms of His love, therefore, you shall be
kept by the hand of His power and, therefore, you shall
never, either finally or totally, fall away.

Christ will make all things work together for your
good, Romans 8:28, "And we know that all things work
together for good to those who love God." Christ has an
endeared love to all you who love God, your love to Him—

being the fruit of His love to you; and when men and devils conspire together to do you harm, Christ's love will turn it unto your spiritual advantage.

Christ will stand by you in trouble and at death, John 14:18, "I will not leave you comfortless; I will come to you." When affliction arises, especially if it is for His sake, and you are bereaved of all outward comforts, Christ will not leave you comfortless. When friends fail, and flesh fails, and heart fails, yes, and life fails—Christ will not fail—but will stand by and strengthen you, and be a light to you in your darkest hours, a stay to your spirits when they are ready to sink within you.

After death, Christ will take care of your souls. He will not allow the devil to seize on them as His prey—but He will send His angels to conduct and convey them into the heavenly paradise that, where He is, there they may be also, Luke 16:22, "And it came to pass that the beggar died, and was carried by the angels into Abraham's bosom." 2 Corinthians 5:8, "We are confident, I say, and willing rather to be absent from the body, and to be present with the Lord."

Christ will raise up your bodies at the last day. If your bodies should be consumed by fire, or drowned in the water, or rot in the earth, whatever becomes of them, the Lord Jesus, at His second glorious appearance, will find them, and raise them, and transform them into the likeness of His most glorious body, John 6:40, "And this is the will of Him who sent Me, that everyone who sees the Son, and believes on Him, may have everlasting life; and I will raise him up at the last day." Philippians 3:20-21, "Our citizenship is in heaven, from which we also eagerly wait for a Savior, the Lord Jesus Christ. He will transform the body of our humble condition into the likeness of His glorious body!"

Christ will send forth His angels to gather you into the society of the elect that have lived in all ages and all parts of the world, and to convey you into His presence to meet Him in the air when He comes to judge the world, Matthew 24:31, "And He shall send His angels, with a great sound of a trumpet, and they shall gather together His elect from the four winds, from one end of heaven to the other." 1 Thessalonians 4:16-17, "For the Lord Himself will descend from heaven with a shout, with the archangel's voice, and with the trumpet of God, and the dead in Christ will rise first. Then we who are still alive will be caught up together with them in the clouds to meet the Lord in the air; and so we will always be with the Lord. Therefore encourage one another with these words!"

Christ will own you, and crown you, and admit you into the kingdom of heaven, which He has prepared for you, Matthew 25:34, "Then the King will say to those on His right—Come, you who are blessed by My Father, inherit the kingdom prepared for you from the foundation of the world!" Here is strong and active love indeed! And shall not the consideration of this love of Christ, raise and heighten your love unto Him? Shall it not provoke and excite you unto activity of love, unto the lively and most vigorous exercised thereof? Has Christ united himself to your nature—and shall not your hearts be united to His person? Has He fulfilled all righteousness for you—and will not you fulfill His command of love? Has He endured such temptations, contradictions, and sufferings, upon your account, and given Himself to die for you—and will not you give your hearts unto Him? Has He risen from the dead and ascended into heaven for you—and will not your affections arise from the earth and ascend into heaven where Jesus Christ is? Does He plead in heaven with the Father for you—and will not you hearken to His pleadings by His Word and Spirit with you for your love? Is He preparing a glorious mansion for you in His Father's house—and will not you prepare a place for Him, and entertain Him in the inner room of your chief affections?

Does, and will, He preserve you in His hand—and will not you embrace Him in your bosom? Will He make all things work together for your good—and will not your affections work towards Him? Will He stand by you in trouble and at death—and will not this put life into your love? Will He send His angels to convey your souls into His presence, when separated from our bodies—and shall not your hearts get to Him and lodge with Him before? Will He raise up your bodies at the last day—and will not the hopes of this raise up your affection? Shall you be caught up in the clouds to meet the Lord in the air, and will Christ there own and crown you—and will not the believing forethoughts of this, ravish your hearts with love to Christ, and transport you with unspeakable joy? The strength of Christ's love to you, methinks, should engage your love for Him, not only in the truth of it—but also in the strength of it!

4. Consider that Christ loves you with the SUREST love. Some friends may love you awhile with some kind of strength and ardency—but such differences may arise between you, as shall soon weaken and cool their love, and of friends they shall prove strangers, yes, become enemies to you. Or, if their love does abide, it is not sure, because they may not continue to live. If their love did not die while they live, they may soon die, and then their love is at an

end; but the love of the Lord Jesus Christ unto you, is the most sure love.

If He begins to love you—He will continue to love you. If He loves you once—He will love you to the end, or rather without end. The love of Christ is not subject to mutations and changes like ours. If you lag in your love—He will not fail in His love. Though you offend Him—He is not irreconcilable. He may, indeed, upon unkindness on your side, withdraw the manifestations of His love for awhile—but He will never wholly remove His love from you.

The love of Christ admits of no changing, knows no ending. Christians, what motives can you find in any person, or anything in the world, which are comparable to those which you have in this Lord Jesus Christ? He is a person most amiable in Himself; His greatness, His holiness, His wisdom, His faithfulness, His fullness, His kindness, all make Him shine with an admirable luster. His relation to the Father, and the love which the Father bears to Him, His relation unto you, being your Shepherd, your Captain, your Teacher, your Advocate, your Sovereign, your Benefactor, your Brother, your Husband, your Redeemer. All these commend Him to your love; but when matchless beauty and loveliness meet in a person that bears matchless love to you: when this most amiable Lord Jesus loves you with such a free love, such a sure and constant love; when His love is incomparable, surpassing all other love, and incomprehensible, surpassing all knowledge, O! With what activity, ardor, and constancy, should you love so suitable an object!

The third sort of motives to excite your love unto Christ, may be drawn from the consideration of Christ's BENEFITS. If you are true Christians, you have:

(1) spiritual light from Christ;

(2) spiritual life from Him;

(3) the pardon of sin from Him;

(4) the robes of righteousness from Him;

(5) the peace of conscience from Him;

(6) the joys of the Holy Spirit from Him;

(7) the riches of grace from Him;

(8) the dignity of children from Him;

(9) the spirit of prayer from Him;

(10) title to the kingdom of heaven, with the first fruits and foretastes of it from Him here, and you shall be put into the possession of it by Him hereafter.

1. You have spiritual LIGHT from Christ. Christ is the Sun from whom all the beams of this light come. Time was, when you were not only in the dark, you were darkness; but Jesus Christ enlightened you, Ephesians 5:8, "For you were once darkness—but now are you light in the Lord—walk as children of light!" It is Christ who has turned you from darkness to light, that has translated you out of darkness, into His marvelous light. He has caused a marvelous light to shine into your minds, whereby He has revealed to you

the wonderful things of the law, that thereby you might discern the odious nature of sin. By this also, He has revealed to you the wonderful mysteries of the gospel, that thereby you might discern the excellency of gospel-privileges, and the exceeding riches of God's grace and kindness through Jesus Christ. Christ has opened your eyes to see the chief evil—that you might be delivered from it, and the chief good and happiness—that you might attain unto it. And does not this light which you have from Christ, call for your love? If the man that was born blind, and was cured of his natural darkness by Christ, loved Christ for this favor so as boldly to plead for Him before the Pharisees, though for it he was cast out of the synagogues, as you may read in John 9—how much more reason have you to love Christ, who has cured you of your spiritual darkness which, had it continued, you would have gone blindfold to hell, where there is blackness of darkness forever!

2. You have spiritual LIFE from Christ. You were spiritually dead—and Christ has quickened you, Ephesians 2:1, "You has He quickened, who were dead in trespasses and sins." We read that Christ raised Lazarus from the dead after he had been buried four days, John 11. Lazarus loved Christ before but, no doubt, this resurrection of him, so wonderful, endeared his love to Christ exceedingly. And shall not Christ's raising you up from you spiritual death—raise your hearts unto a great height of love to Christ? You will greatly love one who is instrumental to save your natural life, when in great hazard and danger, especially if he should do it by venturing his own. And will you not greatly love Christ who has given you spiritual life, which is far more excellent than natural life? He died that you might live, and, if you had not received this spiritual life

from Him—you could not have escaped eternal death in hell.

3. You have the PARDON of sin from Christ. This pardon Christ has purchased for you—and the purchase has cost Him dearly, even His blood, which was of more worth than the treasures of ten thousand worlds—were there so many! This pardon, Christ has sued out for you by His intercession at the right hand of God. While you were under the guilt of sin, you were bound over by the justice of God to suffer the vengeance of eternal fire; but, being pardoned, your obligation to future punishment is taken off, and you are no more liable to wrath to come, and the vengeance of hell—than if you had never sinned! And will you not love the Lord Jesus Christ, who has procured for you, so great a privilege? We read of one who had much forgiven her—and she loved much, Luke 7:47, "Her many sins have been forgiven; that's why she loved much!" And have not you had much forgiven? Have not your sins been very numerous and very heinous? And has Christ obtained the pardon of them all? And will not you love Christ much?

4. You have the robes of RIGHTEOUSNESS from Christ. You are born naked of original righteousness, and you could not work out any real righteousness for yourselves, which might cover your nakedness. The filthy rags of your own righteousness were polluted and defiled—and could not cover you. But Christ has given you the robes of His perfect righteousness to cover and adorn you and, therein, you are accepted as perfectly righteous in the sight of God! O how should we love the Lord Jesus for this garment! If your bodies were naked, and one should give you clothes to cover you, especially if they were rich clothes, you would love such a person; and will you not love the Lord Jesus Christ, who has given you a garment to

cover your souls, and that a very rich one, even the robes of His most pure and unspotted righteousness which, by faith, is put upon you!

5. You have PEACE of conscience from Christ. This is that peace which the Scripture tells us passes all understanding, Philippians 4:7. It passes all understanding to know the worth of it. Such as have this peace would not leave it upon any account. They would part with their estate, or liberty, or life—rather than part with their peace! And those who have it not—but now slight and neglect it—when they are come to the confines of eternity, then they would value this peace, and would give all the world (were it at their disposal) for it. This jewel of peace which you have from Jesus Christ—He has purchased it for you. "The punishment that brought us peace, was upon Him, and by His wounds we are healed," and He has promised and bequeathed it in His last will and testament unto you, John 14:27, "My peace I leave with you, My peace I give unto you." In His reconciling you unto God, He has laid a foundation for this peace in all who are true believers; and if He has moreover spoken peace to you, in giving you well-grounded evidences of your reconciliation. If, after raising a storm, He has sent a calm into you in the testimony of His Spirit to and with your spirits, so that your peace is made with God—O how should this draw forth your love to Christ!

6. You have the JOYS of the Holy Spirit from Christ. We read of the Thessalonians, that they received the Word in much affliction, with joy of the Holy Spirit, 1 Thessalonians 1:6. Such are those joys spoken of in the text—which are unspeakable, and full of glory. These are not carnal joys—but spiritual, which are of a higher nature and sweeter relish, which have a higher object, and are the

beginnings of eternal joys. If you have these joys in any measure, you have them from Christ. He sends the Holy Spirit from heaven to be your Comforter, to fill your hearts with spiritual joys—and shall not your hearts then be filled with love to the Lord Jesus, who is the Author of them!

7. You have the riches of GRACE from Christ. If any of you were poor and ready to starve with hunger and cold, and a rich man should give or send to you a chest full of gold and priceless jewels—would you not love such a benefactor? The Lord Jesus has given you the riches of grace—the least measure of which, is really of more worth than the vastest treasures of gold and precious jewels which ever was gathered together and heaped up by the most wealthy man who ever lived upon the face of the earth! And will you not love Jesus Christ, who has given you these inestimable riches!

8. You have the DIGNITY of children from Christ. 1 John 3:1, "How great is the love the Father has lavished on us—that we should be called children of God! And that is what we are!" This privilege of adoption is bestowed upon you, not only by the Father—but also by the Son, John 1:12—"but as many as received Him, to them gave He power to become the sons of God, even to those who believe on His name." We read of some raised from the dust, and lifted up from the dunghill, to sit with princes, Psalm 113:7-8. It is a far higher advancement, to be lifted up from the dunghill of sin, and of slaves of lusts, and children of the devil—to be made the sons and daughters of the Lord Almighty! This honor have all the saints, and it is Jesus Christ who has conferred this honor upon you, and will not this endear your love to Christ!

9. You have the spirit of PRAYER from Christ, being sons. The Spirit of the Son is sent down into your hearts, whereby you are enabled to say, "Abba Father!" Galatians 4:6. Through Christ, you have access unto God by the Spirit, Ephesians 2:18. It is the Spirit of Christ, who helps your infirmities in prayer, who forms your petitions, who enables you to pray with faith, and life, and fervor. Through Christ, you have free admittance to the throne of grace. Through Christ, you have assistance by His Spirit to pray in prayer. Through Christ, you have a heavenly audience, and gracious returns. O how are you indebted unto Christ! And how should you love Him!

10. You have a title to the kingdom of HEAVEN from Christ. Through Christ you are God's children; and through Christ you are heirs of God, and joint heirs of Christ. It is Christ who gives the first fruits of the heavenly Canaan, the pledge of the future treasure and inheritance which He has promised, and the foretaste, sometimes, of those soul-ravishing pleasures which the saints shall have in fullness, and to eternity, when they are received up into glory. And it is Christ who hereafter will give possession unto you of the kingdom of heaven!

At the day of His glorious appearance, after He has owned you before the whole world of angels and men, and honored you to be His assessors in His judging and condemning the wicked—He will receive you with acclamations of joy and triumph into the glorious palace of the New Jerusalem, where you shall have the beatific vision and fruition of the glorious Jehovah, and be made partakers of such glorious felicity as has not now entered into your hearts to conceive! And will not the consideration of all this—set your hearts on fire with love to Christ!

Christians, is there any person like Christ's person? Is there any love like Christ's love? Are there any benefits like Christ's benefits? No! No! He is incomparable in all. I think, then, you should by this time, feel your love to Christ like fire to burn within with a vehement flame! I think your love to Christ should be like water, I mean the waters of the sanctuary spoken of in Ezekiel 47:3-5 which at the entrance were but to the ankles, a little further were up to the loins, a little further a deep river over the head, where a man might swim! I think you should perceive an increasing of your love under these various motives. If your love were more shallow at first, I think, by this time, it should have got some depth. When such winds blow, the waters should flow and overflow. I think your love to Christ should be raised to a high tide—and run with a strong stream! Thus for the motives drawn from the consideration of Christ's benefits, all of which are so many orators for your love!

The fourth and last sort of motives to excite your love to Christ—may be drawn from the consideration of that love which Christians have, or should have, unto Him. And here consider:

(1) the duty of loving Christ;

(2) the privilege of loving Christ;

(3) the honor of loving Christ;

(4) the wisdom of loving Christ;

(5) the excellency of loving Christ;

(6) the necessity of loving Christ;

(7) the usefulness of loving Christ;

(8) the delightfulness of loving Christ;

(9) the attainableness of love to Jesus Christ.

1. Consider it is your DUTY to love Christ. If it is your duty to have a natural affection unto parents and children; it is much more your duty to have spiritual affections unto Christ. If it is your duty to have marital affection unto your earthly husband and wife; it is a greater duty to have marital love unto this your heavenly Husband. If it is your duty to love brethren, sisters, and kindred that love you, it is a greater duty to love Jesus Christ, who loves you above all relations. It is your duty to love Christ, who is your best Friend.

It is the will of your heavenly Father that you should love Christ. The devil would have you hate Him—but God would have you love Him; and whether it be more reasonable that you should obey the will of God or the will of the devil, you judge. It is the will of Christ that you should love Him. The will of the flesh is against this love—but whose will ought you to comply with? You are not debtors to the flesh that you should obey its command, neither are you debtors to any creatures to give them your choicest affections—but you are debtors unto Christ, to give Him your chief love. Christ has most right to your love, and will you not give to Christ His due? If you are bound to give men their due, are you not much more bound to give unto Christ His due? Christ's due is your best, and have you anything better than your hearts to present Him with? Will Christ accept anything at your hands should you withhold from Him your hearts? Had you thousands of rams, and ten thousand rivers of oil to offer Him; had you all the treasures of the earth at your disposal, and should you lay it down all at His feet, it would be all slighted and disregarded by Him if you give away your hearts.

2. Consider it is your PRIVILEGE that you may love Christ, that Christ will give you leave to do it, and kindly accept your love. Should beggars fall in love with princes in order to the marriage union, both their people and love would be rejected with scorn, anger, and disdain. There is a far greater distance between you and Jesus Christ than there is between the highest prince and the meanest beggar; and yet the Lord Jesus Christ gives you leave to love Him with a spiritually marital love in order to the nearest spiritual union and conjunction; and, notwithstanding His greatness and your baseness, He is not ashamed to give entertainment unto your love. Although you are so mean as creatures, and have been so vile as sinners—yet He does not scorn and disdain you—but both people and love may find ready acceptance with Him. It is your duty to love Christ because He commands you; and it is your privilege that you may love Christ because He allows you to do it.

3. Consider it is your HONOR to love Christ. The real honor of any is not the noble blood which runs in their veins, the high lineage from whence they are descended, the great titles with which they are invested, or the most eminent earthly dignities unto which they are advanced. The heathen could say, "Our stock and noble ancestors, and what we have not done and deserved ourselves, we can hardly call our own." And, "Virtue is the only true nobility." And the Scripture tells us, that the vilest men are exalted, Psalm 12:8, and that the Most High rules in the kingdom of men, and gives it to whoever He will, and sets up over it the basest of men, Daniel 4:17.

Princes and nobles, by their vices and wickedness, may render themselves more vile than the earth under their feet, more base than the mire in the streets. The Word of God accounts only those to be truly honorable that are truly gracious; and this grace of love to Jesus Christ puts a great honor and luster upon all those who have it. There is no greater and higher object for your love than the Lord Jesus Christ, a person of so great eminency and excellency. The love of Christ ennobles the heart; and none in the world have such truly great and generous souls as those who have the greatest love to Him. According to the spirit, so is the man, either base or honorable; and according to the chief love, so is the spirit. If your heart chiefly loves any inferior things, as all sublunary things are, hereby you are debased and dishonored. If your heart chiefly loves Christ, who is a superior good and superlatively amiable, hereby you are dignified and become truly honorable. We read of hope (that is the grace of hope) that it makes not ashamed, Romans 5:5; and the same may be said of this grace of love to Jesus Christ. It makes them ashamed. The covetous will be ashamed of their love of riches, and the voluptuous will be ashamed of their love of pleasures, and the ambitious will be ashamed of their love of honors. Disappointment of happiness and true contentment will make all ashamed of their inordinate creature-love, especially when they come to reap the bitter fruit of their sin in their everlasting punishment, Romans 6:21, What fruit had you then in those things whereof _you are now ashamed, for the end of those things is death? But the love of Christ does not make ashamed; it is no matter of dishonor and, therefore, there neither is, nor will be, matter of shame for any to love Jesus Christ with the greatest strength and ardency. If the wicked despise and scorn God's people upon the account of this love, their scorns are their real glory as, on the contrary, their esteem of any upon the account of sin is a real shame and dishonor.

4. Consider it is your WISDOM to love Christ. Deuteronomy 4:6, Keep, therefore, and do them, for this is _your wisdom and understanding in the sight of the nations, which shall hear these statutes, and say, Surely this great nation is a wise and understanding people. None have such wisdom and understanding as those who have and keep this statute and commandment to love the Lord Jesus Christ, Psalm 111:10, The fear of the Lord is the beginning of wisdom; a good understanding have all they that do His commandments.

The fear of the Lord and the love of Christ are always in conjunction, or rather the former includes the latter. This is the beginning and chief part of wisdom, and those have the greatest understandings who have the strongest affections to the Lord Jesus Christ. The love of Christ is the most reasonable and, therefore, the most wise love. That love is most reasonable which is chiefly carried forth towards that object which is most suitable, and really most amiable and object as the Lord Jesus Christ, as appears in what has been already said concerning Christ's person, Christ's love, and Christ's benefits. Such as love other people or things with a chief love are mistaken in the objects of their love; they apprehend more excellency and desirableness in them than really is in them, and so their love is foolish and unreasonable, there being nothing worthy of it, nothing really amiable in the chief place, beneath and besides Christ.

Such as make choice of Christ for the object of their chief love make the wisest choice. There are really those excellencies in Him which they apprehend and conceive.

They are fools that are slow of heart to love Christ, and they are more wise that are most forward unto this love. It is your wisdom to love Christ chiefly and to love Christ ardently; such wisdom as will make your faces shine in the eyes of good men, and which will put a luster upon your spirits in the eyes of God. True wisdom does not consist in the invention of curious and quaint notions, in the framing of sound and rational deductions, in uttering the sense of the mind in neat and florid expressions; but the chief wisdom lies in the right placing of affections, and none have attained so high a pitch of true spiritual wisdom as those who have attained the highest pitch of love to Jesus Christ. It is a matter of great wonder when there is the greatest reason and the strongest arguments for the love of Christ, that men of the greatest parts and learning, who have heard of Christ, do not readily fall in love with Him and attain higher degrees of this love than others of a more inferior capacity; but the Scripture must be fulfilled, Matthew 11:25, 1 thank You, O Father, Lord of heaven and earth, because You have hid these things from the wise and prudent, and have revealed them unto babes. Such of you as are but babes in worldly wisdom and human learning, as have but mean natural parts, and no improvement by education—yet if you love the Lord Jesus Christ above all people and things in the world, you are far more wise than the greatest scholars that are without this love.

5. Consider the EXCELLENCY of this love unto Jesus Christ. As the knowledge of Christ is the most excellent knowledge, Philippians 3:8, Yes, doubtless, I count all things but loss, for the excellency of the knowledge of Christ Jesus my Lord; so the love of Christ is the most excellent love. It is a love of the most excellent object, the Lord Jesus, who is so excellent. It is a love of the most excellent original; it comes down from heaven, it

is wrought by the Spirit of God. It is a love that renders them most excellent that have it. The wicked that are without this love are like dross; the righteous that have it are like gold. The wicked that hate Christ are like dirt; the righteous that love Him are like jewels. Other loves darken and defile, the love of Christ brightens the spirit and renders men truly illustrious, the excellent of the earth.

6. Consider the NECESSITY of this love unto Jesus Christ.

(1) The love of Christ is UNIVERSALLY necessary. Some of you need to do this thing, and others of you need to do that—but all of you have the greatest need to love Christ. Some of you need this friend, and to love him that you may keep him: and others of you need another friend. One friend cannot serve the necessities of all—but all of you need Christ for your friend. He is the only friend who can serve all your necessities, and you need to love Him above all friends. It is necessary that you who are poor should love Christ, who have but few or no friends: and it is necessary that you who are rich should love Christ, who have many friends, Christ being a friend instead of all to them that have the most.

(2) The love of Christ is ABSOLUTELY and INDISPENSABLY necessary. It is not necessary that you should climb up and ascend to Jesus Christ, who is above; it is not necessary that you should abound in wealth, that you should have full bags and full coffers, and much riches in your houses; but it is absolutely necessary that you should have riches of this grace of love to Jesus Christ in your hearts. Food is not so necessary to satisfy your hunger, clothes are not so necessary to cover your nakedness, houses are not so necessary to shelter you from the injury

of the weather. The most needful thing is not so necessary to your bodies as this love to Jesus Christ is necessary to your souls. You may be poor and in the lowest condition here on earth, and yet be happy while you live, and eternally happy in the other world if you have this love to Jesus Christ; but, without this love, whatever your riches and honors and friends, whatever your earthly delights and enjoyments are, though ever so desirable, ever so plentiful—yet you are miserable and shall be miserable. You may love other people and things in the world subordinately—but you must love Jesus Christ chiefly, otherwise you are under the curse both of the law and gospel, and you cannot escape the vengeance of hell.

7. Consider the USEFULNESS of this love unto Jesus Christ.

(1) The love of Christ is useful in PROSPERITY to ballast the heart so that it is not overset with the full gales of a flourishing condition. It is of use to moderate the affections to lawful things, and it is of use to keep the heart from unlawful and sinful loves. If Christ does not have your hearts, some base and foolish lusts will have them, which will wound your consciences with guilt and pierce your hearts through with many sorrows.

(2) The love of Christ is useful in ADVERSITY to bear up the heart from sinking and being overwhelmed with the winds and waves of trouble and affliction. It is of use to establish the heart from being extraordinarily moved in the most stormy times. Not only faith—but love too, is of a fixing nature, to keep from amazing fears of evil tidings and the greatest perils; and of a strengthening nature, to stay and support the spirit, and keep off pressing griefs and despondencies in the darkest and most doleful days.

(3) The love of Christ is useful to quicken and excite unto DUTY. This makes the yoke of Christ easy, and will enable you to draw therein. This makes the burden of duty (so accounted by the most) to be no burden in esteem. If you have much love unto Christ, you will account duty to be your privilege and the service of Christ to be freedom; and none of His commands will be grievous—but all of them joyous unto you. If you have much love unto Christ, your hearts will be inflamed thereby with zeal for your Master's glory, and you will never think you can do too much for Him.

(4) The love of Christ is useful to arm you against TEMPTATIONS. If faith is a shield, love to Christ is a breastplate against the sharpest darts which the devil can throw at you. Love to Christ garrisons your hearts against this enemy, and is a strong defense against any overtures which the devil may make in his temptations to draw you to sin. "How can I do this evil and offend my dear Lord?" will be the answer of love to repel temptations to sin, whatever alluring proffers they may be accompanied with. Temptations will have no force to prevail over you if this love of Christ is strong within you.

(5) The love of Christ is useful to fit you for the CROSS, and the greatest SUFFERINGS which you may be called unto for the sake of Christ. If you have great love to Christ, you will be ready to suffer for Christ with patience and with cheerfulness; the heaviest cross will seem light, disgrace and shame will be counted honor, losses will be esteemed gains, pains pleasures, or, at least, privileges. Prisons will seem palaces, and death will be accounted life. O how have some run to the stake, and embraced the flames of fire kindled to burn them, when they have felt the

fire of love to Christ burning strongly within them! Thus this love is useful in life.

(6) The love of Christ is useful at DEATH. This love in its strength will put a beauty upon the aspect of death, which seems so grim and terrible unto the most. If you have much love to Christ, you will look upon death as Christ's messenger, sent for you, to bring you out of the dark prison of the world and the body, and to convey you unto the mansions of glory where your dear Lord is, and you will not be unwilling to leave the world that you may live with Christ.

8. Consider the DELIGHTFULNESS and sweetness of this love unto Christ. If there is sweetness in the love of the head, if there is delight and comfort in the love of Christ's disciples for their Master's sake, there is much more delight and comfort in the love of Christ Himself, the Master, for His own sake. The apostle tells us of comfort in love, Philippians 2:1, that is, in the love one of another— but the consolations in the love of Christ are far exceeding. There are no such sweet motions of heart as those of the strong and fervent outgoings of it in its love to Christ, especially when Christ draws near, and manifests His love unto the soul.

Christ rejoices in His love unto His disciples, and they may rejoice in their love to Him, and this joy in the love of Christ is full joy. John 15:11 says, These things have I spoken unto you, that My joy might remain in you, and that your joy might be full. In the former verse, Christ speaks of His love to them, and here of His joy in them. They were the objects of His joy as they were the objects of His love, and, according to the measure and strength of their love to Christ, so is the fullness of their joy in Christ. Song of

Solomon 1:9 says, You have ravished my heart, my sister, my spouse; you have ravished my heart with one of your eyes, with one chain of your neck. These are words of Christ the beloved unto His spouse, the Church, expressing the ravishing delight which He found in her looks of faith, or glances of love, and the chain of graces which she was adorned withal. How, then, may your hearts be ravished with unspeakable delight in looking upon Christ's most amiable face, and in the fervent acting of your love unto Him! When a glance of His eye, a smile, a beam from His countenance, kindles a fire in the breast, and this fire of love to Christ burns and flames; O how sweet is this flame beyond what tongue is able to express!

9. And, lastly, consider the ATTAINABLENESS of this love to Christ. Brutes are not capable of this love to Christ—but you are capable. As your minds are capable of knowing Him, so your hearts are capable of loving Him. Others have attained this love, who were as much without it, and as much averse unto it as any of you may be. Here you are capable; hereafter, if you live and die without it, you will be utterly incapable. You have now the means of grace and, as of other graces, so of this grace of love to Christ, in the diligent use of the means, you may attain thereunto. Thus I am done with the motives to excite you unto the love of Christ.

The second thing propounded in the prosecution of the use of exhortation, was to give DIRECTIONS. The directions will be of two sorts:

(1) how to attain this love to Christ;

(2) how to show this love to Christ

First, how to attain this love to Christ. And here I shall:

(1) Direct you how you may attain this love to Christ in the truth of it, where you are wholly without it.

(2) Direct you how to attain much of this love to Christ, where you have it but in a low degree and weak measure.

The first directions, then, shall be how you who are graceless and Christless, and wholly without this love to Christ—may attain true love to Christ.

Direction 1. If you would attain this love unto Jesus Christ, whom you have never seen, you must get a thorough persuasion that there is such a person as Jesus Christ, and that He is such a person indeed as the Scriptures have revealed Him to be. The reason why heathen are without love to Christ—is because they have never heard of Him. The reason why many who have heard of Christ are without love to Him—is because they are not really persuaded that there is, or ever was, such a person as Jesus Christ in the world. If you would attain this love, you must give a firm assent to this truth (which is the greatest of all, and the very pillar and foundation of the whole Christian religion), that Christ really is, and that the history of Him is no cunningly devised fable.

If you have reason to believe that there was such a person as Alexander the Great, that there was such a person as Julius Caesar, both of whom lived before Christ's time, you have more reason to believe that there was and is such a person as Jesus Christ. You have only secular history for the former—but you have also sacred history for the latter.

You have only the writings of men to testify the one—but you have the Word of God in the holy Scriptures to testify the other. You have as much reason to believe the history of the gospel —as to believe any other history; and you have more reason to believe the history of the gospel than to believe any other history. I shall suggest one reason among many, which might be mentioned.

The history of the gospel was believed by as learned men as any in the world, in and near the time of their writing; which belief some of them sealed with their blood, which they would never have done had they found any reason to suspect the truth of this history, which (had there been any reason of suspicion) they might easily have found out in those times, if such a grand fable as this could not possibly have gained credit among wise and inquisitive men; especially when it would have been their greatest worldly interest, the preservation of their estates and lives, to have disbelieved and disowned it.

If, beside the Apostles, all the learned church fathers (whose works are extant among us, who lived near the apostles' times, and some of whom suffered martyrdom for Christ's sake) saw reason to believe that there was such a person as Christ, surely you have reason to believe, and no solid reason to discredit the report of Him in the history of the gospel. And, when you have attained a firm assent unto this, get a full persuasion that Jesus Christ is such a person as the Scriptures record and testify Him to be. Be persuaded of His personal excellencies—His amiableness, His greatness, His holiness, His wisdom, His faithfulness, His fullness, His kindness. Be persuaded of the relation He stands in to the Father, His only begotten and dearly beloved Son, the relation He stands in to His people, especially in His offices of Prophet, Priest, and King, as I have set Him forth in the motives to stir up love. Acquaint yourselves with the history of His birth—so wonderful, of His life—so holy, of His works—so powerful, of His doctrine—so heavenly, of His sufferings—so great, of His death—so painful (and yet so voluntary), of His resurrection, ascension, session and intercession at the right hand of God—so needful for us, as you have this history upon record in the New Testament. The assent to this in your minds, will be a preparative for the attaining of true love to Jesus Christ in your hearts.

Direction 2. If you would attain true love unto Jesus Christ, you must get conviction of SIN, and a sense of your NEED of Christ. The prevailing love and relishing of sin, is inconsistent with true love unto Jesus Christ. Such as love Christ hate sin; and such as love sin have an enmity against Christ. While your hearts go after your covetousness or your wickedness, your hearts cannot be set upon Christ.

Before you can love Christ, your hearts must be taken off from sin. Get, therefore, a conviction of sin as the greatest evil in the world. Be persuaded what an evil and a bitter thing it is, to transgress God's law and, thereby, to affront the high Majesty, the great King of glory! Look into the Word of God—and see what is there required, and what is there forbidden; and then look back upon your lives, or look into the register of your consciences, that you may find out what your sins of omission and commission have been. Take a view of your transgressions of the law, and of your disobedience also unto the gospel; and, as you are guilty before God, so labor for a clear sight and deep sense of your guilt; how you are under the curse for your disobedience, how you are liable to ruin and eternal destruction for your sins!

Look upon sin as the most evil and harmful thing in the world. If there is any evil in any temporal calamities which befall men; yes, if there is any evil in future miseries, in the extremity and eternity of hell's plagues and punishments, be persuaded that there is far more evil in sin, which is the cause of all. Think how miserable you are, while under the guilt and reigning power of sin; that the worm is not so vile—as your sins; that the toad is not so full of deadly poison—as your sins; that the filth of the earth is not comparable unto the filth of your sins! Think how base and hypocritical you have been! Think how monstrously ungrateful to your Maker and Benefactor! Think what traitors and rebels you have been to your Supreme King and Sovereign!

Think what peril and danger you are continually in— of death and hell! Think how weak the thread of life is, which ties soul and body together, which may be suddenly cut when you are least aware, when you are most secure; and then, if you are found in a Christless state, your souls will be conveyed immediately unto a place of remediless and eternal misery! Be persuaded, that you are irrecoverably undone—unless the Lord Jesus Christ saves you, that you cannot escape the dreadful vengeance of God—but must be tormented most horridly and everlastingly among the devils and the damned in hell— unless the Lord Jesus Christ delivers you from the wrath which is to come!

The sight and sense of sin, your miserable condition thereby, and of your indispensable need of Christ, will make way for your love of Him.

Suppose that you were in great debt unto a severe creditor, and had not one penny to discharge it, and you were threatened by him to be thrown into prison where you must lie and rot, starve and die, without hopes of relief or release—unless you could make payment of the debt. And if you should hear of such a rich man who was willing and offered to be your surety and to pay all for you—surely you would have an endeared love to such a friend and benefactor.

Just so, your sins are debts beyond the vastest sum of money that ever was owed or paid—and you are not able to pay one farthing, to give the least satisfaction unto God unto whom you are indebted. God is strictly just, and, without full satisfaction to His justice, will throw you into a worse prison than the most nasty dolesome prison on earth! I mean, into the prison of hell—where you must lie without the least relief or any hopes of release! The Lord Jesus Christ offers to be your surety, to pay off all for you, and to give you a full discharge. Were you sensible what a debt sin is, and what a prison hell is—surely it would work your hearts into an endeared love of such a friend and surety who alone can keep you out of this dolesome dreadful prison, into which without Him, you will certainly, and may suddenly—be thrown!

If any of you were sick of a death-threatening distemper, and you had made use of many physicians but none could do you good; and if you should hear of one physician who could assuredly, and would readily and freely cure your disease and save your life—surely you would thankfully make use of this physician, and his kindness would exceedingly engage your love. Just so—sin is the soul's sickness; you are sick unto death. Sin, when it is finished, will bring forth death, not only temporal—but eternal. It is the Lord Jesus Christ alone, who can cure you of this deadly sickness, who can remove your sin and, thereby, deliver you from this death of deaths. Get a sense of the dangerous sickness of sin—and you will prize, and use, and love the Lord Jesus Christ, who is the only physician of value in this case!

If any of you were guilty of murder, or theft, or high treason, or some other heinous breach of the law of the land—for which you were apprehended, arraigned, accused, and condemned to be hanged or burned, or to a more tormenting death than either; and if you should hear of a prince at court that had begged the pardon of such crimes for such malefactors and had obtained it, and should he send to you to signify his willingness to do the like for you—surely you would thankfully accept of such a offer, and would love this prince as your life, who should thus preserve you from death! Just so—you are all guilty of high treason and rebellion against the King of heaven in your breach of His law, and you are condemned by this law, not to be hanged for it or beheaded—but to be burned for it—to be burned in the fire of hell, which is unquenchable! The Lord Jesus Christ is the Prince of glory, a friend in the court of heaven, who has procured a pardon for many such malefactors, and sends to you to signify His willingness to procure your pardon if you will make use of Him. Surely, if you have a sense of your crime and danger—you will apply yourselves unto Christ to save you—and you will not withhold your love from such a one as should show you such unparalleled favor!

Direction 3. If you would attain true love unto Christ—you must get a saving interest in Christ. You must lay hold on Christ by faith, so that you may be united to Him and related to Him. It is faith which works love. To those who believe, Christ is precious! But, by unbelievers, He is slighted and cannot be loved. Without union to

Christ, you will have no affection to Christ. The foundation of love is laid in the relation to the beloved. And this union to, and interest in, Christ—is only by faith. If, then, you would embrace Christ in the arms of love, you must first lay hold on Christ, and receive Him by the hand of faith. Whatever motives and attractions of love there are in Jesus Christ, there will be none to you without this saving interest and relation.

Christ is most beautiful, most lovely and amiable—but He will not be so in your eyes—as long as you are without the eye of faith. He is great and powerful—but so much the worse for you because, without a saving interest in Him, His power is engaged against you! He is pure and holy—and while in your sins, you are, therefore, the more odious in His sight. He is wise and knows all things, therefore, He is privy to all your sins. He is most true, and therefore, will fulfill His threatenings against such as go on still in their trespasses. He is full—but you, without a saving interest in Him, have no share in His fullness.

He is kind—but it is to those who are related to Him; but what is this to you who are unbelievers? He is a Shepherd to His sheep—but you are goats! He is a Captain to His soldiers—but you are enemies! He is a Teacher to His disciples—but you are the devil's scholars! He is a gracious Sovereign to His subjects—but you are rebels! He is a Priest to His people, having made atonement for their sin, and makes intercession for them—but you trample His blood under your feet! He is a Friend and Benefactor to His people—but you are strangers! He is a Brother and a Husband to His people—but you stand in none of these relations! He is a Redeemer to His people—but you are slaves and captives to Satan!

The light which He gives is most sweet—but you are darkness. The life which He imparts is most excellent—but you are dead in sins and trespasses. He gives pardon of sin—but you are under guilt. He gives peace of conscience—but your consciences are still wounded and seared. He gives the joys of the Holy Spirit—but you are in danger of eternal woes. The robes of His righteousness are most rich—but you are naked. The riches of His grace are inestimable—but you are still poor. The dignity of being made the sons of God is most admirable—but you are children of the devil. He gives access unto God in prayer—but you are still at a distance. He gives a title to the kingdom of heaven—but, if you continue in your present state, you will be shut at last out of the palace which is above—and be thrust down into the prison of hell which is below!

What, then, are all these motives to draw forth love to Christ? It is union and relation unto Christ, and saving interest in Him by faith—which puts life into these motives, that they may indeed attract love. O then, be persuaded, without further delay, to endeavor after this saving interest in Christ! You must have it or you are lost irrecoverably; and you will be miserable eternally! Yet you may attain this interest. Others have attained it who are as evil and as vile as yourselves; and you are called unto Christ. O be persuaded, then, to come unto Christ, and join yourselves by faith unto Him, so that you may have a saving interest in Christ, and in all His benefits!

If you ask "What is this faith, which gives a saving interest in Christ? What it is to believe?" I answer out of John 1:12 that it is to receive Christ; "To as many as received Him, to them gave He power to become the sons of God, even to those who believe on His name." Be persuaded, then, to receive Christ, and accept Him upon the terms of the gospel. Receive and take hold of Christ by the hand of faith and, that you may do this:

(1) You must let go your hold of SIN. If you hug sin in your bosom, if you harbor base lusts in your hearts—you cannot receive and give entertainment to Christ there. You must thrust sin out—if you would let Christ in!

(2) You must let go your hold on the WORLD. I do not say you must let it go out of your hands, and throw away the estates which God has given, unless you are called to leave all rather than to forego Christ or any of His truths; but you must let the world go out of your hearts. The world must not sit upon the throne of your hearts; that seat must be reserved for Christ. Chief love and inordinate love to the world and things in the world, must be taken off.

(3) You must let go your hold of SELF. Your own righteousness and all self-confidences must be parted with! You must be humbled and emptied of yourselves—if you would be prepared for the receiving of Jesus Christ, and receiving of that fullness which there is in Him.

And then, receive Jesus Christ as your High Priest to reconcile you unto God, trusting alone in His merits and mediation. Receive Jesus Christ as your Prophet to instruct and lead you in all truth by His Word and Spirit. Receive Jesus Christ as your Sovereign Lord and King to rule you. Receive Jesus Christ as your Captain to tread down your spiritual enemies under your feet. Receive Jesus Christ in all His relations of Shepherd, Friend, Brother, and especially in the relation of a Husband; and join yourselves to Him, and make over yourselves to be guided, guarded, provided for, and governed by Him. This is to receive

Christ, and this is to believe. This gives union, and relation, and saving interest in the Lord Jesus. And if you do thus join yourselves to Christ by faith, you will quickly feel love to Christ to spring forth, to work and act, and that vigorously; and to bring forth such fruit in the life as shall evidently show that love to Christ is rooted in the heart!

Direction 4. If you would attain true love unto Christ—be diligent in the use of all those MEANS which God has appointed for the working of it. I shall instance only in two means:

(a) Be diligent in hearing the WORD preached. As faith comes by hearing, so love to Christ is wrought by the same means. "Hear, and your souls shall live!" said the Prophet, Isaiah 55:3; and, I may say, "Hear that your hearts may love!" The ears may affect the heart with love to the Lord Jesus. While Lydia was hearing Paul preach, her heart was opened, Acts 16:14, and while you are hearing ministers preach of Christ, your hearts may be opened to receive Him and to embrace Him in the arms of your dearest love. See Acts 11:15, "As I began to speak, the Holy Spirit fell on them!" While Peter was preaching, and the Gentiles were hearing—the Holy Spirit was sent down from heaven and fell upon them. Just so, while you are hearing the Word, God may give forth His Spirit, to work this grace of love to Jesus Christ in your hearts.

(b) Be diligent and earnest in PRAYER unto God for this love. Confess and bewail before Him your lack of this love; tell Him you deserve a double anathema because you do not love Christ; and, withal, tell Him you cannot, of yourselves, love Him, that you can as easily lift up a mountain to heaven—as lift up your hearts unto Christ; but that you desire that He would draw up your love to Christ by His Spirit. Beg Him that He would put out the fire of lust, and all inordinate creature-love, and that He would kindle a fire of love in you to this most lovely Jesus, which no corruption in your hearts may be able to extinguish! And, in your prayers, present your hearts to the Lord Jesus. Offer them up freely to Him, and desire that He would accept them, that He would take hold of them and take possession of them, and erect His throne in them as an everlasting habitation for Himself.

How to attain great degrees of love to Christ. Having given directions how you may attain the truth of love to Christ—I come now to give directions how you may attain much of this love to Christ, where you have it but in a low degree and weak measure. Would you attain much love to Christ?

Direction 1. Be much in holy contemplation of Christ. Consider often what motives there are of love in Him. Press them upon your spirits, and labor to awaken and rouse up your hearts unto the vigorous exercise of this love. Spend time in secret retirement, and there think and think again of the superlative excellencies and perfections which are in Christ's person—how wonderful and matchless His love is, what heights which cannot be reached; what depths in it, which cannot be fathomed, what other dimensions which cannot be comprehended!

Meditate often on His benefits, how incomparable His love-token is; and, while you are looking, you may feel your hearts leaping. While you are taking a view of Him, before you are aware, your hearts, like the chariots of Amminadab, may run unto Him! O the ravishments of love! The transports of soul, which some believers have found in their retired thoughts and views of Christ!

Get often into the mount of divine contemplation—and there look upwards unto heaven and think with yourselves, "Yonder, yonder, above the shining sun—is the more glorious Sun of righteousness. There, at the right hand of the throne of God, is my beloved Jesus, and though He is so high above me, both in place and dignity—yet He thinks upon me, and pleads for me, and many a gift has He sent and, by His Spirit, conveyed unto me; and I can ask nothing of the Father in His name but, if it is really for my good, I have it by His means."

"O dear Jesus, how lovely are You in Yourself! The darling of heaven! The delight of the Father! The admiration of angels! O what brightness of glory, what shining luster are You arrayed with! You are clothed with most excellent majesty and honor! You are girded with infinite might and power! The beauty of Your face is most wonderful! The smiles of Your countenance are most sweet and delightful!"

And does this lovely beauteous one, this fairest of ten thousand, this most excellent and altogether lovely person—bear a special love to me? To such a vile worm as me! To such a dead dog as me! To such an undeserving, ill-deserving, hell-deserving sinner as me! O what marvelous kindness in this! What infinite riches of free grace! Does He know me by name? Has He given Himself for me, and given Himself to me—and shall not I give Him my heart! Am I written in His book, redeemed with His blood, clothed with His righteousness, beautified with His image! Has He put the dignity of a child of God upon me, and prepared a place in the Father's house for me! O how wonderful! O how astonishing!

What shall I render unto Him? What returns shall I make? Had I a thousand tongues—should I not employ them all in speaking His praise! Had I a thousand hearts—should I not present them all, as too poor for a thank-offering unto Him! And yet am I slow—slow of heart, to love this dear and sweet Jesus! Awake, O my soul! Awake from your dullness and stupidity! Shake off the sleep which glues your eyelids so close together, shake out the dust of the earth which has gotten into your eyes, and keeps you from the view of your matchless Beloved! Arise, O my soul, and lift up yourself; unfetter the feet, unclog yourself, take the wing, and mount up above the sky and visible heavens, even to the place where my lovely and dear Jesus is! Take your leave of the world and all things therein. Bid farewell to the flattering honors, the deceitful riches, the glancing pleasures that are here below! Bid adieu to them, and leave them to those who place their chief happiness in them!

If earth had your body for awhile—yet let it have your heart and chief affections no more. Come, O my soul! Ascend, and soar aloft unto the heaven of heavens. The way unto the Holy of Holies is accessible. The veil is torn asunder, the Forerunner has entered, and you may also have entrance, too, with your thoughts, and desires, and loves, and hopes, and joys. There you may see, and view, and admire, and embrace your dearest Lord. There your heart may find a fit object for its love, even your dearest Lord Jesus, who will not reject and despise you—but give kind entertainment unto your love, and withal give the fullest and sweetest returns! There your heart may find a room to dispose of itself, and not only a lodging like that of a wayfaring man for a night—but a habitation wherein to dwell and to take up its eternal abode. Let your heart be your forerunner so that, when your body drops off from you, you may know where to take yourself, and find ready entertainment there where your heart has been long before.

Why do you hang downwards, O my soul? Why do you bend so much to the earth and earthly things? What is there here below—which is not beneath you and altogether unworthy of your love? How empty and vain and thorny are these worldly things? Do not waste your time—and weary yourself for every vanity; do not sting and wound yourself with these things anymore. What ails you, O my soul, that you are so backward to the love of Christ? Is it because you cannot see Christ with the eyes of your body? You shall see Him with those eyes hereafter, when He comes in His glory, and your body is raised and repaired, and fitted to bear such a sight! You cannot see the wind— but you hear its noise and feel its blasts; and do you not hear Christ's voice in His Word? Do you not feel the breathings of His Spirit in His ordinances? You are invisible yourself, O my soul, and are you so drenched in flesh that visible objects shall have more power to draw down your heart than this most glorious object (though now invisible) shall have power to draw up your heart? Do you question and doubt His love to you, and does this dampen and discourage your affection?

Whose image is this which is engraved upon you? Is it not the image of Christ? What writing is that upon your heart? Is it not God's law written by Christ's Spirit? Whose deckings and adornings have you got about you? What beauty is this which is put upon you? Is it not Christ's loveliness! Where did you get those bracelets, that ring, those jewels, that chain of graces? Are they not Christ's love-tokens which He has given you—and yet will you doubt His love?

If you feed corruption strong—yet do you not receive some grace, although it is weak? Have you not some love to Christ, although it is low? Are not your desires chiefly after Him, which evidences that your chief love is to Him? And is it so with any but such whom Christ loves? Does not Christ love you first—and yet will you question His love? Banish, then, your fears; silence your doubts, O my soul! Rouse up yourself—and climb up by Jacob's ladder, which is let down to you from heaven, and settle your love upon Jesus Christ and those things which are above where Christ sits at the right hand of God. Such retired contemplations of Christ, and soliloquies, and pleadings with your own souls, when alone by yourselves, will tend exceedingly to the promotion of your love unto Christ.

Direction 2. Would you have much love to Christ? Be much in reading and studying the Scriptures! The Scriptures are a looking-glass, in which Christ may be seen. He cannot be seen face to face in this world; this is the happiness of the triumphant church in heaven, not of the militant church upon earth. What may here be discerned of Christ, is in the looking-glass of the Scriptures and gospel ordinances. This is that looking-glass spoken of in 2 Corinthians 3:18, "We all, with open face, beholding, as in a glass, the glory of the Lord, are changed into the same image, from glory to glory!" Christ is the glory of the Lord, the brightness of His Father's glory. Would you have much love to Him? Be often looking, viewing, and beholding Him in the looking-glass of the Scriptures! By much beholding of Him, you may be transformed more and more into the likeness of His holiness, and into the likeness of His love—which is glory begun.

The Scriptures have the image of Christ engraved upon them; the image of the Father is upon the Son, and the image of the Son is upon the Scriptures. There you may see the picture of Christ, the beauty of Christ; at least some lineaments are there drawn by the hand of God, although not fully, and to life. I mean, such you will see in Him when you come to behold Him face to face in heaven; yet His beauty is drawn is such proportions, and with such shadows, as you are now capable of beholding.

Would you have much love unto Christ, whom you have never seen? Look much upon His picture and image in the Scriptures. The Scriptures are Christ's love-letters. In the second and third chapters of Revelation, Christ sends seven epistles to the seven Asian churches. There are many epistles and love-letters, as it were, in the Scriptures, especially in the New Testament, wherein Christ gives most kind expressions of most endeared love unto His people. Read much and study Christ's love-letters, especially those parts of the Scriptures wherein Christ expresses most of His kindness and love. Read often and consider such places, Let the Word of Christ dwell richly in you—and this will feed and maintain your love to Christ. This is a means to have Christ dwell in your hearts not only by faith—but also by the most endeared love.

Direction 3. Would you have much love to Christ? Be much in prayer to God for this love, Ephesians 6:23, "Peace be unto the brethren, and love, with faith from God the Father." Not only peace is from God, who is called the God of peace, and not only is faith from God, who works it by His almighty power—but also love is from God, who is the God of love. He circumcises the heart to love Himself and to love His Son. This love of Christ is a grace of the Spirit which God freely gives and powerfully works. The beginnings of it, the increase of it, all the measures and degrees of it—are from Him. If you would attain high measures of love to Christ, you must apply yourselves unto God in prayer, and therein seek diligently to Him for it. If you would have much love to Christ in your hearts, you must be often at the throne of grace upon your knees, and there humbly acknowledge if not the lack—yet the weakness, of your love to Christ. Bewail your sins which dampen your affections, and earnestly request that He would work your hearts unto a strong love. Be importunate in prayer for this.

Follow God day by day with the same requests; plead with Him for it. Fill your mouths with arguments, and fill your arguments with faith and fervent desires. Tell Him, whatever loveliness and love there is in Christ, whatever attractions to draw forth your love—yet of yourselves you are utterly unable to put forth the least motion of true affection unto Christ. Tell Him that this love to Christ, though it is your duty—yet it is His gift; that you ought to act it—but this you cannot do, unless He works it. Tell Him how easily He can kindle this fire of love to Christ in your bosoms and blow it up into a flame. Tell Him He has bid you to ask and you shall have; and whatever you ask according to His will He hears, and that it is His will you should love Christ not only truly—but also strongly.

Tell Him that you desire much love to Christ, and that these desires come from Himself and, therefore, earnestly desire the fulfilling of them. Tell Him that, if you do not love Christ much, you shall be apt to overlove the creature, which will be displeasing to Him. Therefore, request that you may have such a love to Christ as may overpower all other love, and keep your hearts from all inordinancy of love, to anything beneath and besides the Lord Jesus Christ. Plead how much it will be for His glory—that you should have much love unto Christ, that hereby you shall be enabled to honor Him all the more in the world. Plead how much it will be for your good. Tell Him that if you asked for wealth and honors, and creature delights in abundance, they might be a snare to you, and for your hurt; but a strong love to Christ is needful and useful, and you can be sure it will be for your good. Urge His promise of circumcising the heart to love Him, and plead His faithfulness. And, if you are thus importunate in prayer for much love to Christ, and will not be denied—you shall not be denied.

Direction 4. Would you have much love to Christ? Get much faith. Faith works love both to the Father and to the Son. According to the measure of your faith—so will the measure of your love be. Such as are without any faith in Christ—are without any love to Christ. Such as have but a feeble faith in Christ—have but a weak love to Christ. And such as have the strongest faith in Christ—have the strongest love to Christ. The strongest faith gives the clearest discovery of Christ's infinite excellencies and perfections. It is not the eye of sense which discerns Christ, neither is it the eye of reason which discerns Him. Whatever discoveries we have of Christ are by revelation, and this is discernible only by faith. Faith is the evidence of things not seen, and the unseen Christ is evident by faith to be the most excellent person, and the most suitable object of love; and the more evident the object of love is, the stronger will the love be.

Moreover, faith is not only the eye of the soul to discern Christ—but also the hand of the soul; not only to take hold of Him—but also to receive from Him of His fullness, grace for grace and, by consequence, more of this grace of love to Him. Our communion with Christ is by faith; the more intimate acquaintance and fellowship we have with those whom we love—the more endeared will be our love. The strongest faith brings us unto the greatest intimacy, fellowship, and familiarity with Christ, and therefore, it is a means of the strongest love. Endeavor, then, to get a strong faith, and to live daily in the powerful exercise thereof. The more you live by faith—the more you will dwell in the love of Christ.

Direction 5. Would you have much love unto Christ? Labor for much of the Holy Spirit; labor for much of the light of the Spirit. There must be not only the looking-glass of the Scriptures and the eye of faith—but also the light of the Spirit that you may have a clear discerning of this lovely Lord Jesus. Labor for much of the operation of the Spirit. The Spirit is like wind to blow up the sparks of love in your hearts into a flame. Labor for the indwelling of the Spirit, and that the promise may be made good to you which Christ gives to His disciples, John 14:16-17, "And I will ask the Father, and He shall give you another Comforter, that He may abide with you forever; even the Spirit of truth, whom the world cannot receive, because it sees Him not, neither knows Him: but you know Him, for He dwells with you, and shall he in you."

Direction 6. Would you have much love unto Christ? Labor for clear evidences of His love unto you. The apprehensions of Christ's loveliness may excite to some love—but the full, well-grounded persuasions of Christ's love to you will, above all, heighten your love to Christ. Doubts of Christ's love cause fears—and fears contract the heart, and therefore, are opposite to love which is the expansion and enlargement of the heart. Perfect love casts out fear; the more love—the less fear; and the more doubts and fears—the less love. Such as doubt much of Christ's love to them, may love Christ truly—but they cannot love

Christ strongly. You will love a less lovely person who loves you—more than a more lovely person who hates you. The love of the person beloved is a most amiable qualification and strong attraction, yes, one of the greatest incentives and inducements unto love. Get, then, a persuasion of the infinite love to you of this infinitely lovely Person—that you may be able to say with Paul, Galatians 2:20, "Christ loved me, and gave Himself for me!"

Look diligently into the Word of God, and find out the characters there, of those who are beloved by Christ; and then look diligently into yourselves and see whether your face will not answer that face in the looking-glass of the Scriptures. See whether you can find the lineaments of the new man within you; whether you have experienced a gracious change. Is there now spiritual light—where there once was darkness? Is there now love to God—where there once was hatred to God? Is the the Law of God now written on your heart—where once the law of sin commanded all? Is the bias of your wills and heart, now God-ward, Christ-ward, and heaven-ward; which, heretofore, was only sin-ward, earth-ward, and hell-ward?

Pray earnestly unto God that He would give you a full assurance that, if you are indeed effectually called, if you are indeed united and related unto Jesus Christ, you may know it and no longer doubt thereof.

In a word, seek diligently after the manifestations of Christ's love in all the ways of His ordinances. Do not rest in the externals of the ordinances—but seek after Christ in the ordinances. Follow Him from ordinance to ordinance, and always be looking for Him and looking towards Him—until He turns about and looks upon you, and gives you His

gracious smile. Seek and wait for that manifestation of
Himself—which He has promised to those who love Him,
John 14:21. Wait for His mission of the Holy Spirit from
heaven, 1 Peter 1:12, to shed abroad the sense of His love
to your hearts, Romans 5:5; and, if you knew assuredly, and
had a sense hereof given unto you by the Spirit of Christ—
O the joys which you would then have in Him! O the love
which you would then have to Him! As your joys would be
unspeakable, so your love would be unspeakable also. Such
a warmth of heart and burning of love to Christ, you would
feel within you as is beyond the rhetoric of the tongue to
set forth!

Direction 7. Would you have much love to Christ? Get
much hatred of sin; and accordingly, watch, pray, strive,
and fight against sin as the worst of evils, as that which so
much displeases your Lord. Bewail sins of daily incursion,
and labor that your sins of infirmity may be less every day.
Take heed of sins of sudden surprise—but chiefly of
designed sins, and that you do not comply with any
temptations unto grosser miscarriages which, like water
cast upon the fire of your love to Christ, will put out the
flame, and leave only a few unperceivable sparks in the
corner of your hearts. Do not allow sin to have any room in
your hearts or, if it will abide and you cannot thrust it quite
out, let it not have a quiet habitation within you.

Disturb sin as much as you can; wage war every day
with your remaining lusts. Let no day pass over your heads
without giving some blows, some thrusts and wounds to
sin. The more room sin has in your hearts—the less room
Christ will have there. Particularly, take heed of inordinate
love to the world, and the things in the world, the
prevalence of which love will dampen your love to Christ.
By how much more the world gets of your love—by so

much the less Christ will have of it. A subordinate love you may have to people and things in the world—but let no person or thing have your chief love, only Christ. Love nothing for itself with a superlative love—but love all inferior things with inferior love; love all under the Lord and in the Lord, and for the Lord's sake. Get all inordinate affections to the world crucified by the cross of Christ! You must having dying affections to perishing things—if you would have a living and strong love to the ever-living Jesus!

Direction 8. Would you have much love unto Christ? Associate yourselves most with those who have most love unto Christ. You may fetch light from their light, and you may fetch warmth from their fire; dead coals are kindled by the living, and your dead hearts may be kindled with love to Christ by the warm discourse of those who have warm hearts. Be ready to speak of Christ and for Christ in any company as you have opportunity, and diligently watch for an occasion. Shut your ears against profane and filthy communication. Do not listen to discourse which is vain and frothy; be ready to begin and promote that discourse which is serious and savory, that which is gracious and may tend to your own and others edification. Study and practice the art of provoking all whom you converse with, not unto strife and contention—but unto this love and affection unto the Lord Jesus Christ; and, while you are endeavoring to warm others with this love, you may be warmed yourselves!

Direction 9. And, lastly, would you have much love unto Christ? Be much in the exercise of this love; hereby it is increased and heightened. If you exercise this love frequently, it will hereby get strength and activity. Every day endeavor to put forth some vigorous acts of love unto

Jesus Christ. In your ordinary callings, secular businesses and employments, you may send up some looks of love unto Jesus Christ in frequent short prayers; but especially, in the duties of God's immediate worship. Labor that your love may flow out unto Christ most vigorously. In your daily secret devotion and family worship, let love to Christ draw forth tears from your eyes, at least cause grief and sorrow in your hearts, in the acknowledgment of your sins, whereby He has been dishonored and displeased.

Let love to Christ draw forth earnest desires after Christ—and those communications, manifestations, and consolations which He gives to none but such as are His. Let love to Christ put requests into your mouths, arguments into your requests, and fervor into your arguments, in your pleadings with Him at the throne of grace for further supplies of His grace, and that you may be brought into more intimacy of acquaintance with Him.

Every day you should express your love to Christ, especially on the Lord's day, when almost the whole day is to be spent in public and private exercises of pious worship, and all your love to Christ should be in exercise. In your attendance upon Him in ordinances, you must bring not only your bodies before Him—but present your hearts unto Him. This you should be careful to do in public prayer and hearing of the Word, preaching, and singing psalms. Often should you endeavor, in every ordinance, to lift up your hearts unto the Lord; but, above all, when you approach the Lord's table, all your graces should there and then be in exercise, especially this grace of love to Jesus Christ. Your eye there should affect your heart when you see the representations of your crucified Lord, and think what manner of love He bore to you, that He should submit Himself unto such a death for you. How should this affect your hearts! And, if ever, then your love to Christ should show itself and act with the greatest vigor and strength!

Having given directions how to attain true and strong love to Christ; I come now to the last sort of directions how you should SHOW your love to Jesus Christ.

More generally, show your love to Christ in your OBEDIENCE unto Christ. John 14:15, "If you love Me, keep My commandments." Be faithful in the performance of all known duties which Christ commands, and be careful in the forbearance of all known sins which Christ forbids. Let your great care be to please Christ, whoever is displeased; and your great fear be of offending Christ, whoever is offended with your strictness. Show your love to Christ:

(1) in the sincerity of your obedience;

(2) in the willingness of your obedience;

(3) in the universality of your obedience;

(4) in the constancy of your obedience.

1. Show your love to Christ—in the SINCERITY of your obedience. Hypocrites will do some things which Christ commands—but it is from carnal motives and with carnal designs. But love to Christ must be the motive, and the honor of Christ must the end—of all sincere obedience. Obey Christ because you love Him, and with a design to please Him. What you do, do heartily unto the Lord, and above all things, desire and endeavor that what you do, may

be pleasing to Him, 2 Corinthians 5:9, "We make it our aim to please Him."

2. Show your love to Christ in the WILLINGNESS of your obedience. Some will obey Christ—but it is with great reluctance. They will perform duties—but they are burdensome, a weariness, and toilsome, and the commandments of Christ are grievous unto them. They are scarcely ready to perform any duty—until they are scourged unto it by the rods of affliction, or spurred and pricked forward by the goads of conscience. O the listlessness and indisposition in most professors, unto the most spiritual part of the service of Christ, which is an evident proof of the defect of love, either in the truth of it, or at least in the measure and degree of it! Let your love show itself in the willingness of your obedience. Serve the Lord with a willing and ready mind, with alacrity and cheerfulness of spirit, looking upon the service of Christ as your honor, and esteeming every duty as your privilege.

If you have any constraints upon obedience—let them be constraints of love, as 2 Corinthians 5:14. If you are forced to obey Christ—let there be no violence but the violence of love; if you are dragged to duty—let it be with no other cords than the cords of love. Let love be the spur and goad to urge you forward—that you may not only walk but run in the ways of Christ's commandments with an enlarged heart.

3. Show your love to Christ in the UNIVERSALITY of your obedience. Hypocrites will perform some duties which are for their good, and which will serve their carnal designs. Other duties they omit and totally neglect. But let your love to Christ reveal itself in your obedience to all His commandments. Though you cannot here attain perfection

of obedience—yet let your obedience be universal. Obey Christ not only in open duties, which men are witnesses of—but also in secret and spiritual duties which depend upon the exercise of the heart and mind—such as meditation, contemplation, self-searching, and prayer; as also in the spiritual part of all duties, which no eye can be witness unto, but the eye of God. Hereby you may be distinguished from all hypocrites in the world.

4. Show your love to Christ in the CONSTANCY of your obedience. Galatians 5:7, "You did run well, who hindered you, that you should not obey the truth?" Some hypocrites are zealous professors for a while, and at first setting out seem to outstrip many who are sincere—but they soon tire and are weary not only in well-doing—but of well-doing. They quickly stumble and fall, and not only fall down—but fall off; not only fall back—but fall away, and turn into fearful apostates. Show your love to Christ—not only in setting out well—but in continuing your Christian course well, unto the end of the course of your lives. Begin well and patiently continue in well-doing. Persevere in your obedience, "Be not weary in well-doing, knowing that in due time you shall reap, if you faint not," Galatians 6:9. And, if you are faithful unto death, Christ has promised to give you the crown of life! Revelation 2:10.

More particularly, show your love to Christ:

(1) in your learning, keeping, asserting, and maintaining of Christ's truths;

(2) in your public-spiritedness and zeal for Christ's honor and interest;

(3) in your vigorous resistance and opposition of Christ's enemies;

(4) in your following of Christ's example;

(5) in your readiness to take up and patiently bear Christ's cross; and

(6) in your desires after Christ's presence here, and longing for Christ's second appearance at the last day.

1. Show your love to Christ—in your learning, keeping, asserting, and maintaining all of Christ's truths.

(1) Learn Christ's truths. Acquaint yourselves by diligent reading of the Scriptures and other books which may be a help thereunto, with all fundamental truths of the Christian religion in the first place—and so go on and proceed farther to learn those truths which are in the Scriptural superstructure. And whatever truths you find a foundation for in the Scriptures, which are the Word of truth, receive them not only in the light of them—but also in the love of them. If the branches of Scriptural truths are in your heads, and the leaves of them in your profession, and the fruit of them in your actions—let the root of them be in your hearts.

(2) Having learned the truths of Christ as they are in Jesus, let them not hang loose in your understandings—but keep them fastened and fixed in your minds. Hold the truths of Christ fast, prize them above all jewels; do not part with them upon any terms. Let all go: estate, liberty, and life itself, rather that any of this rich treasure which Christ has entrusted you with!

(3) Assert the truths of Christ. Do not be ashamed or afraid to own any truths of Christ, in the most adulterous and gainsaying generation. Profess your belief in Christ and His truths; endeavor that the light of these truths may shine abroad, and cast forth such bright beams in the dark world where you live—that others may be brought hereby unto the knowledge of the truth.

(4) Endeavor to maintain Christ's truths. Earnestly contend for the doctrine of faith once delivered to the saints, endeavor to convince gainsayers, and to defend Christ's truths against those corrupt and erroneous opinions and doctrines which, like leaven, is very apt to spread and infect the minds of men.

2. Show your love to Christ—in your public-spiritedness and zeal for Christ's honor and interest. Let your affections be public—not private, narrow, contracted, and centering in self. Let your love be a public and general love. Love not only relations—but love all Christ's disciples, though of different persuasions and interests, because of the image of Christ. And love not only your friends who love you—but also your enemies who hate you, because of the command of Christ. Let your desires be public desires. Desire the welfare of the universal church, and of all God's people throughout the world; and, accordingly, pray for their peace and prosperity. And endeavor, as you have opportunity, to promote the public good, more that your own private advantage. Seek not your own things—but the things of Jesus Christ.

Let your grief be public grief. Grieve not only for your own sins—but also for the sins of others whereby Christ is dishonored in the world. Grieve not only for your own afflictions—but also for the afflictions of all believers,

Hebrews 13:3, Remember those who are in bonds, as bound with them; and those who suffer adversity, as being yourselves also in the body. You are in the same mystical body with all Christ's afflicted members; and when some members suffer—the rest should suffer too by way of sympathy, bleeding in their wounds and grieving in their sorrows.

Be also ready to relieve any, especially Christ's disciples, when they are in distress and need, according to your capacity, and as you have opportunity. Employ all your talents for your Master's glory, and endeavor to promote the interest of the Lord Jesus unto the utmost of your abilities in reference to those who are without. If you are called yourselves, labor to call others unto Christ, as Andrew called Peter, Philip called Nathaniel unto the Messiah, John 1:40-45. If you have found the Messiah, or rather have been found by Him, let your love to Christ, and love to souls, prompt you to endeavor the conversion of others that are your relations, your friends, and acquaintances.

Put your unconverted friends in mind of their miserable estates while under the guilt and reigning power of sin, while slaves to the devil and their own lusts. Remind them of death and the fearful consequences thereof, to all unpardoned sinners. Tell them of Christ, that He is the only Savior and Redeemer of mankind; how able and willing He is to save them if they seek after Him and apply themselves unto Him. Tell them that not long ago—that you were in the same state with themselves, living in the practice of the same sins, and going on in the same way to destruction; and that the Lord has showed mercy unto you in your conversion, bringing you into a state of salvation. Tell them that there is mercy also for them if they look after it; that

God's grace is most free, His mercy most plentiful, that Christ is most gracious and casts out none who come unto Him. Tell them of the amiableness of Christ's person, of the surpassing love which He has shown to fallen mankind in His dying for them; and that, though He was dead—yet He is alive, and lives for evermore to intercede for all those who make choice of Him, and make use of Him for their Advocate. Therefore, persuade them to break off their sins by repentance, which otherwise will be the ruin both of their bodies and of their souls in hell; and, without delay, to come unto Christ and accept Him upon gospel terms.

If any of you cannot manage these arguments well yourselves, persuade them, if you can, to hear such ministers and sermons as, through God's blessing, have been effectual for your conversion; and thus you may be instrumental to augment the kingdom of Christ, which is one of the best ways of expressing your love unto Christ.

In reference to them which are within, labor to promote the interest of Christ among those who are truly gracious, by vigorous endeavors to strengthen and establish them, to quicken and encourage them in the ways of the Lord. Communicate the experiences which you have had, as you see there is real need, and it may tend not so much to your praise—as your Master's honor. Labor in your places to be both shining and burning lights: be forward to every good word and work. Look upon yourselves as the devoted servants of Christ, and that you are not your own; and, therefore, lay out yourselves to the utmost for Him, and give all diligence to glorify Him with your bodies and spirits, with your estates and interests, with your gifts and talents—all which are His, and ought to be at His devotion.

3. Show your love to Christ—in your vigorous resistance and opposition of Christ's enemies. There are three grand enemies of Christ which you are engaged to fight against, namely, the devil, the flesh, and the world, which war both against Christ and against your souls. This trinity of adversaries combine together against His Anointed, doing their utmost endeavor to break His bands, to untie His cords, and to unhinge His government. They would pluck the crown off Christ's head, could they reach it, and the scepter out of His hand. They would divest Christ, if they could, of all His power here on earth, and confine Him to His territories in heaven; but all their attempts in this kind have been, and will be, in vain. Christ has vanquished them; but still some life and power is left with them, to war against the holy seed.

You are Christ's soldiers, listed under His banner; show your fidelity and your love to your Captain and General—in manfully maintaining your spiritual combat against His and your spiritual enemies. Fight the good fight of faith, resist unto blood, do not yield upon any account. Disdainfully turn away the eye and ear when these enemies would entice and allure you; and stoutly make resolute opposition against them when they most furiously assault you. Hearken to no suggestions of the devil, temptations of the world, or motions of the flesh—which would induce and draw you into ways of sin—or which would force and drive you out of the ways of Christ. Resist, oppose, and labor to gain some victories over these adversaries every day.

Especially get conquest over the flesh—and the other two will be soon vanquished. Christ showed His love to you in submitting Himself to be crucified for you; you must show your love to Christ in crucifying your flesh, with its

affections and lusts, for His sake; in your self-denial and
mortifying the deeds of the body, when you deny your
carnal reason, your carnal wisdom, your carnal will, your
carnal affections, your carnal interest, all inordinances of
your sensual appetite—for the sake of Christ! When you
crush pride, envy, revenge, malice, and all evil lusts—for
the sake and because of the command of Christ—all these
are acts and evidences of love to Christ, and herein you
should exercise yourselves daily.

4. Show your love to Christ—in your following His
example. Reveal your affection unto Him in your imitation
of Him, in writing after His copy, in treading in His steps,
in walking as Christ Himself walked when He was here
upon the earth. Show your love to Christ by laboring after
likeness unto Christ, that you may be like Him both in your
inward disposition and in your outward life. Christ was
humble—you be humble in your own esteem. Christ was
meek—you be gentle, easy to be entreated, and not easily
provoked. Christ loved God—let God be the object of your
love. Christ hated sin—let sin also be the object of your
hatred. Christ condemned the world—get crucified
affections unto it. Christ was compassionate to those who
were in distress—labor for the like affections. Christ used
to worship publicly in the synagogues, to pray with His
disciples, and to spend time also in secret prayer—so you
should give your attendance in the public assemblies of
God's people, worship God in your families, and be often
upon your knees at the throne of grace in secret.

Christ's mind was a heavenly mind—let the same
mind be in you, as was in Christ. Christ's will was
submissive to His Father's will—let the same will be in you
as was in Christ. Christ's words were gracious and
edifying—let your speech be always with grace, savory,

and that which may be for edification. Christ's life was an active life—He was always doing good, and He was exactly holy in all His action. Be active and diligent in the service of God in doing good to others, and be holy as Christ was holy, in all your conduct. Thus should you show your love to Christ in following Christ's example, and in imitating Him in everything wherein you are capable of such imitation.

5. Show your love to Christ—in your readiness to take up and patiently bear Christ's cross. I do not say you should desire sufferings for Christ; but I am sure that strong love to Christ will not allow you to decline them. Do not go out of God's way for them. If you meet with the cross in the way of duty, do not turn back or start aside—but cheerfully take it up and, when you have got it up, patiently bear it and do not throw it off. When it is your duty to suffer for Christ, look upon it also to be your privilege, and be glad for the opportunity, rejoicing that you have anything to part with for the sake of Christ. If it is good name, or good estate, or good friends, if it is liberty or life itself—such expressions of love are very honorable and very pleasing to your Lord and Master.

6. And, lastly, show your love to Christ—in your desires after Christ's presence here, and in your longing for His second appearance at the last day.

(1) Desire Christ's gracious presence HERE and the manifestations thereof so that, according to His promises, He would come unto you, that He would draw near, and that you might feel that He is near. Desire that you might have clearer discoveries of Christ, and more intimate communion and fellowship with Christ, above all company and fellowship. Desire the company, fellowship, and

acquaintance with Christ, that you might walk and converse with Him, and that there might be a daily fellowship between Christ and your souls, and that all distance and strangeness between you Him, might be removed. Let your love express itself in desires after Christ when He is absent, and in delights when He is present. Rejoice in the Lord exceedingly, when He manifests Himself unto you graciously. Admire His beauty and delight in the persuasions of His favor. Let the actings of your love, and the workings of it, be such to your Beloved daily.

(2) Desire also and long for the second appearance of Christ at the LAST DAY. When He says, "Surely I some quickly!" Say, "Amen, even so come Lord Jesus!" Look upon time as slow of heel and wing, because it runs no faster, and flies no swifter. Look to the end of time, and long for it, because then, with these eyes, you shall see Him whom your soul loves; because then you shall see Christ come down from the throne of God with such brightness of beauty as will transport you with wonder and joy.

Say, "When, Lord Jesus, will You take to Yourself Your great power, and clothe Yourself with Your authority and come down to judge the world? When will You open the everlasting gates of heaven, which have been shut so long? When will You descend from heaven with a shout, with the sound of the great trumpet, and send Your angels to gather all Your elect from the four winds—that all who love You may meet in one society? When shall we put on our garments of immortality, and be caught up in the clouds to meet You in the day of Your triumph? When shall the day of our coronation come, and of our admission into the glorious mansions which You have prepared for us in the glorious palace which is above? When will You show us Yourself, and allow us to behold You face to face? When will You show us the Father, and give us to behold Him immediately without a veil? When will You show us Your glory which You had with the Father before the world was, and give us not only to see it—but to share in it? When will You open the treasures of Your love, and receive us into Your nearest, closest, and sweetest embracements, and give us to drink of those rivers of pleasures which are with You? O hasten, Lord, hasten Your glorious appearance, that You may be glorified before the whole world, and we be glorified with You; that we may be then taken to live with You, and reign with You, and be made perfectly happy in the full and everlasting enjoyment of You!"

And what do you now say, after all motives to excite and persuade you to the love of Christ, and directions therein? Shall all be in vain?

What do you say, sinners? Shall Christ have your hearts or not? Will you harbor base lusts in your hearts—which will damn you and keep out the Lord Jesus Christ, who alone can save you? Shall I gain no hearts for Christ by all my sermons which I have preached concerning the love of Christ? My Lord and Master has sent me to woo you, to win your hearts for Him; may I succeed or not? Shall my message be accepted, and Jesus Christ, the most lovely One, find entertainment with you? If any person or thing in the world, which you most dearly love, does so well deserve your love—lock your ears still against all my words, and let them perish like an empty sound in the air. Lock your hearts against Christ, who stands knocking at the door, and give an absolute and peremptory refusal to give Him any room there! But if, in the whole world, you cannot find out a suitable beloved besides Christ; if there is nothing here below, but is unworthy of your hearts; if all inferior things, while they have your chief love, debase and defile you; and, unless your hearts are taken off from them, will certainly ruin and destroy you everlastingly—O then, be persuaded, without any further delay, to open the everlasting doors of your hearts to let Christ into them, and set Christ up in the highest seat of your affections! O be persuaded to give Christ your chief love, to give Him your heart, and your whole heart! With grief and hatred, let go your hold of sin—and embrace the Lord Jesus Christ in the arms of your dearest love!

And then I would say to you as our Savior did to Zaccheus, when he gave Him entertainment in his house, "This day has salvation come unto you!" O happy day unto you! O happy you that ever you were born, if this day Christ is heartily entertained by you! This, then, would be the day of your conversion, in which the angels would rejoice; and, though grief and trouble might invade you for awhile because of your sin—yet this would make way for your spiritual joy. Weeping may endure for a night—but joy would come in the morning! But O the joy which you will then have in the day of your coronation, when all tears shall be wiped away from your eyes, and when you shall have admission into the glorious presence of the Lord, where there is fullness of joy and pleasures for evermore!

And what do you say, believers, you who have some love to Christ? Shall this doctrine, and these sermons which I have preached, be a means to raise and heighten your love? Your love has been too much mixed—will you love Christ more purely? Your love has been very weak—will you love Christ more strongly? Your love to Christ has been but a spark—shall it now break forth into a flame? After such blowings—shall there be no burnings? When you think of Christ's person so amiable, His love so incomparable, His benefits so inestimable—shall not this fire your hearts? And will you not now love Him more dearly and ardently than ever? Will you be persuaded to get off your hearts from earth and earthly things, and get up your hearts to your Lord who is in heaven, and to settle your love there upon Him so as never to withdraw it from Him anymore? Will you love the Lord Jesus much, whom you can never love too much? Will you now dwell in the love of Christ and be more frequent and fervent in the actings of it? Then, O what comfort would you find in your love—and what sweetness in the sense of Christ's love! This would be the surest evidence that Christ loves you; and how would this sweeten your passage through the valley of affliction—and through the valley of death. This would sweeten a bitter cup—and make a sweet cup more sweet.

In life, the sense of Christ's love will be better than life; but at death, this will be the only stay and support which you can have. Nothing else can give any well-grounded comfort in a dying hour. Death rages and plays the tyrant everywhere, shoots his arrows hither and thither. Sometimes he smites those who are older than yourselves, and sometimes those who are younger; sometimes those who are weaker than yourselves, sometimes those who are stronger; sometimes those who are better, sometimes those who are worse. Sometimes the righteous are smitten, sometimes the wicked; sometimes the profane, and sometimes professors; that all might be awakened to prepare!

And what is it which can give you comfort when you come to the border of death? You may have the love of your dear relations, weeping and mourning at your bed-side; children, kindred, and friends, wringing their hands, and looking with a pitiful countenance upon you, grieving to part with you; but what comfort can all their love yield unto your departing soul? Their love may disturb you and make you more unwilling to die and leave them, because they are so unwilling to part with you; but the love of Christ, and the sense thereof, will be a comfort indeed, because He is a friend whom you are not departing from— but going unto. And, O the delight which then you may have, when friends look most sad and death looks most grim, when the trembling joints, the clammy sweats, the intermittent pulse, the rattling throat, and other symptoms, give notice of near approaching death! Then to think, "I am now come, not only to the door of eternity—but also to the gate of my Father's house, where many saints have gone before me, and many angels are attending for me, and where my dearly beloved Jesus is, and has prepared for my reception an eternal habitation! Here are friends about my bedside, waiting for my soul that, as soon as it is loosened from this dying carcass—they may convey me to the heavenly paradise! Within a few

minutes—I shall be with my dearest Lord where my faith will be swallowed up in vision; my hope swallowed up in fruition, and my love

will come to perfection. O the glorious light which there and then will shine in to every corner of my mind! O the love and joy and ineffable delight—when I come to see and enjoy and live forever with my most dearly beloved Jesus!

This, this only, will make you willing to die—and this sense of Christ's loveliness will effectually sweeten your passage though the dark entry of death!

Made in the USA
Columbia, SC
26 February 2020